2009

Lelu and Mitzy engaged in
"a Michelangelo touch."

The Renaissance touch with its
spiritual energy transcending
life ... and history ...

to Elizabeth

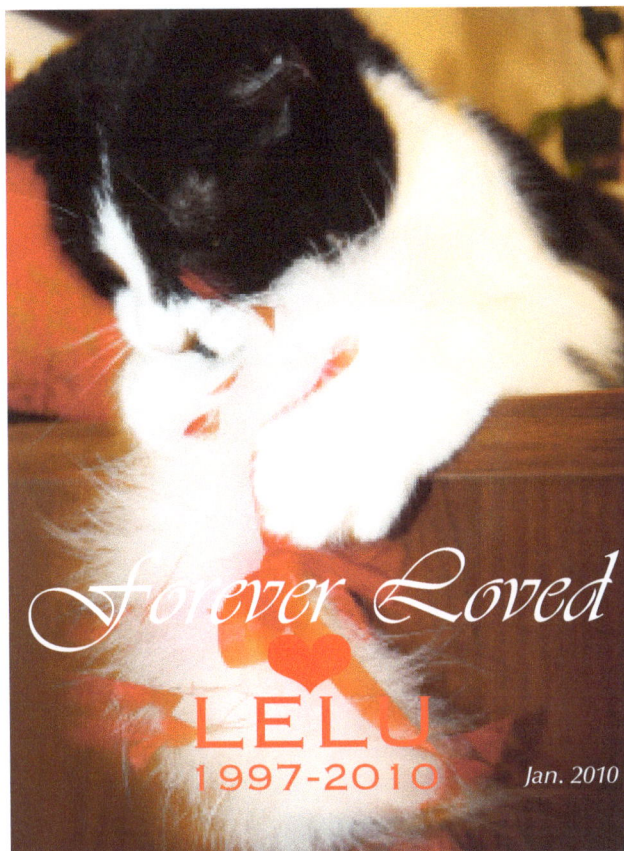

Forever Loved

❤️

LELU
1997-2010

Jan. 2010

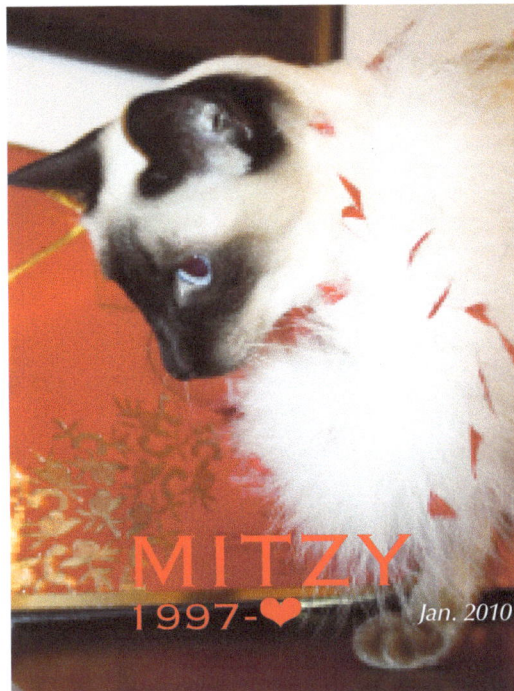

MITZY

1997-❤️

Jan. 2010

Forever Loved is a book reflecting the life and love of Lelu, the Manx
and Mitzy, the Chocolate Point Siamese—from adoption in August 1997
to Lelu's death on February 16, 2010

Forever Loved©
LELU

by Elysse Poetis™
(written in 2010)

PHOTOGRAPHY
Elysse Poetis

DESIGN
Klaus D. Emrich

EDITOR
Elizabeth A. Jordao

First original published in 2010 by
VON DER ALPS PUBLISHING CORPORATION
CANADA
www.vonderalps.com

CANADIAN CATALOGUING IN PUBLICATION DATA

ISBN 978-0-9782302-2-7

Printed in USA

TABLE OF CONTENTS

THE END

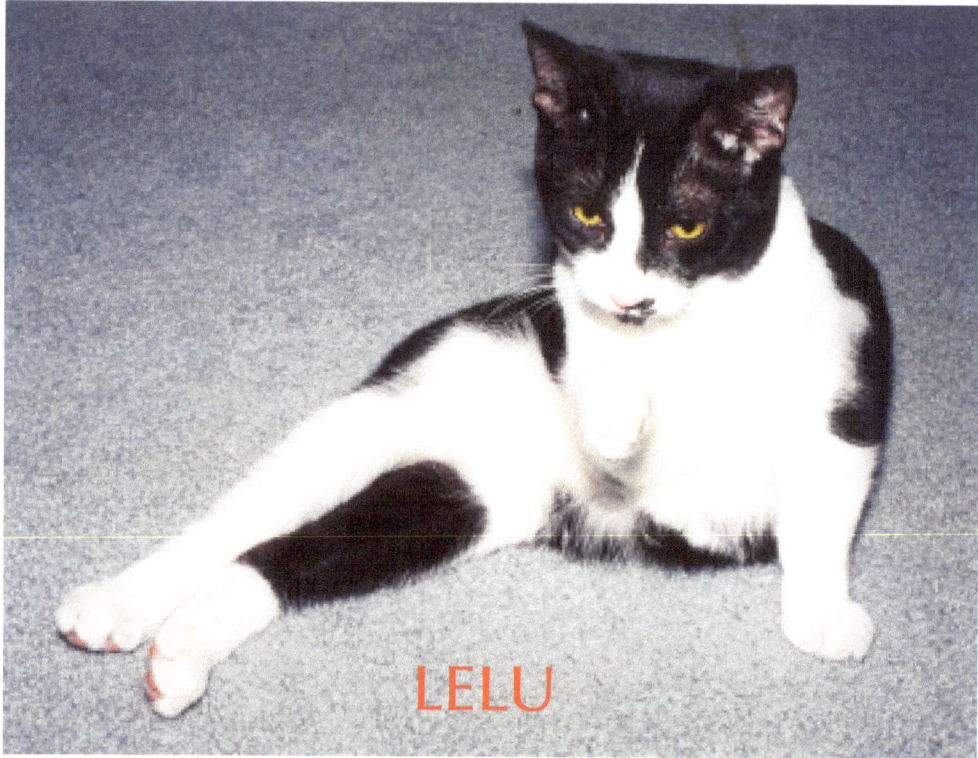

LELU

A FOUR MONTH OLD BABY MANX
ADOPTED FROM THE ANIMAL SHELTER

IN A GARDEN OF FLOWERS, LELU YEARS LATER.

FOREVER LOVED ... LELU

♥

IN LELU'S MEMORY

Years ago I had the privilege of adopting Lelu, a tiny Canadian kitty, a baby Manx found in a ravine, lost or abandoned by some bad people. Days prior my daughter, who was 15 at the time, also adopted a four month old Chocolate Point Siamese she named Mitzy. You can only imagine what happen when I arrived home and introduced them to each other.

Forever Loved is a superb book for children, teenagers and adults. Every page contains pictures that will entertain you to the limits and will also make you stop and reflect. This book is perfect for those wanting to adopt and will have a remedial effect on those who have lost loved pets. Definitely, it is educational for children, and highly recommended as entertainment for seniors.

We shall never forget that some people are irresponsible when it comes to the welfare of our global pets. All media outlets, including the TV and the internet, confirm daily such dramatic realities, making us aware how much needs to be done on behalf of these helpless small friends we should consider family or in many cases, our best companions on Earth.

Our pets have the capacity to love us to such a degree, so faithfully, that it is impossible not to seriously consider their undeniable intelligence. I wrote in my first book that "LOVE is the intelligence of intelligence," or if you wish, "LOVE is the royal blood of wisdom."

In my experience, all my pets loved me. Because I love all life, I'll follow my childhood dream and promote noble behavior, through art. In this life, drama did not spare me from pain and deceit, yet I believe in standing up and fighting for the good and the beauty that are so much needed.

Pets fight, too! To combat human ignorance many animals (birds, dolphins, cats, dogs, horses, etc.) are starting to mimic the human language. Enormous numbers are, and always have been, acting as guides, rescuers, messengers, vehicles and soldiers. All life carries intelligence. That should be the general perception. In fact, love is intelligence à la carte. In 1981, while pregnant, I too was rescued by Canada from a refugee camp near Vienna, Austria. Like Lelu, I was lucky to be adopted.

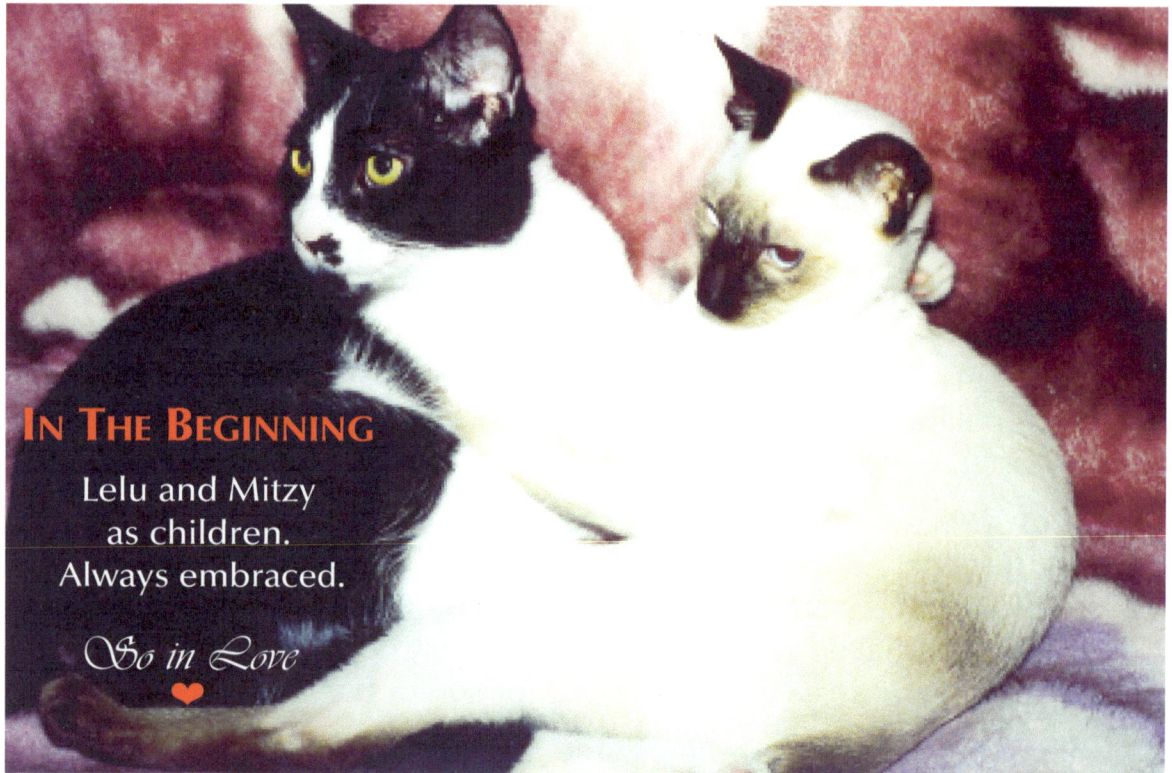

IN THE BEGINNING

Lelu and Mitzy
as children.
Always embraced.

So in Love

♥

IN THE END

Lelu and Mitzy as seniors.
Look at them!

Forever in Love

♥

Mitzu

*Mitzu was born in 1996.
In August 1997 he vanished.*

From the pain of losing him, new love was born—the love for Lelu and Mitzy.

ONCE UPON A TIME ...

A STORY OF LOVE BETWEEN HUMANS AND CATS

Elizabeth, my teenage daughter, dreamed of having a cat. This was in 1996. Since she was my only child, I made her wish come true. But before I tell you the story, I just want to mention that Elizabeth is big now. She has children, a dog, flowers and books. She's made of love. Because I am the photographer and the author of this book, I will tell you the best I can about how Elizabeth's enormous love for animals changed my world forever. Remembering my childhood surroundings back in time (in Europe) with all sorts of animals and people who loved them, I want to emphasize the fact that here in Canada, today, we too love animals very much.

Pets are our friends! They bring us love and laughter. They teach us lessons, patience and compassion. They make us smart. That's why we fall in love with them. That's why when they die, we cry so much.

The story of Lelu and Mitzy began when the lovable Mitzu, Elizabeth's one year old black male kitten, vanished. We never found him, so, we adopted Lelu and Mitzy.

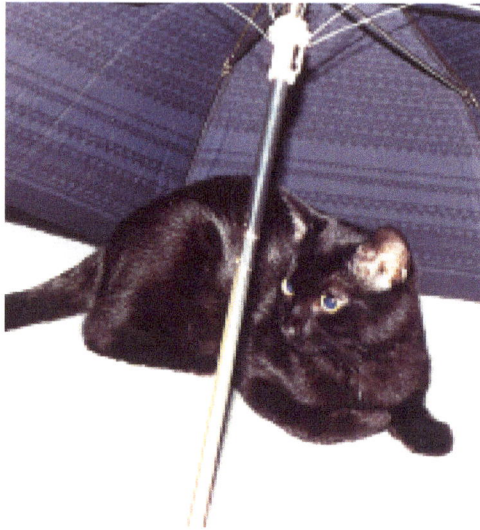

IT ALL STARTED WITH ELIZABETH'S LOVE FOR MITZU, HER ELEGANT BLACK CAT.

♥

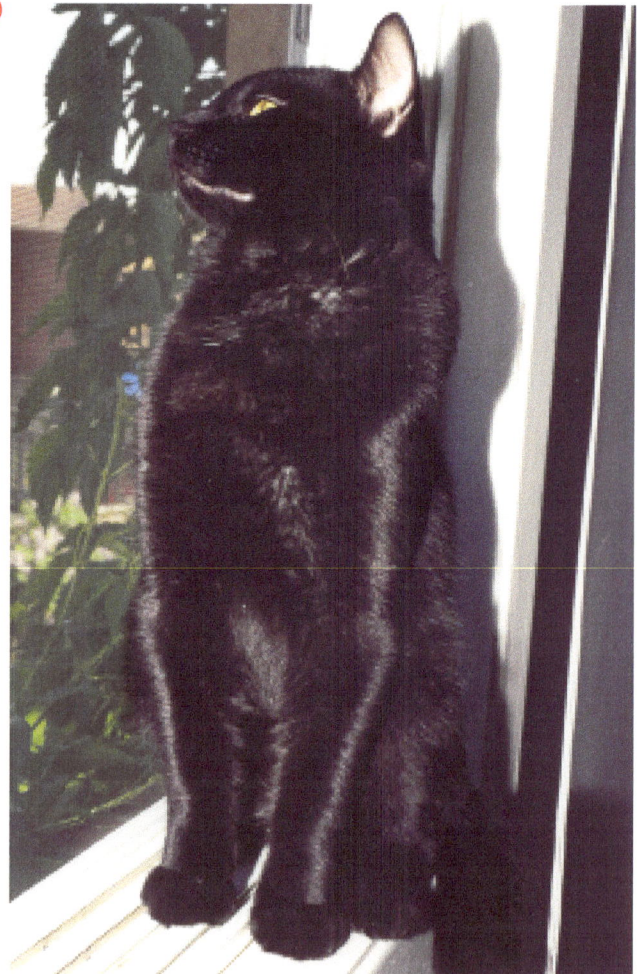

The big drama started in August 1997, after Mitzu's disappearance. Just one year prior she had purchased him from the pet store in Square One Shopping Centre, the famous city of Mississauga. Elizabeth has enormous love for cats. This kitty was quite small and visibly fragile, and I suggested to her not to take him. I sincerely thought that he might not survive, not to mention my fear of trauma resulting from such devastation. But Elizabeth, stubbornly stood her ground and told me that she is not leaving the store without this tiny beautiful black kitty.

We took him home. We loved him. We nurtured him, and he grew into a very fine and strong kitten. Often when he was relaxing, his tail would create a special display, like a french braid. What a wonderful cat! We would let him outside, always supervised and wearing a collar indicating his name, address and telephone. Mitzu loved our neighbour's children. Sadly, late one evening as he was playing outside, Mitzu took off while courting a young female cat. This was the week we planned to neuter him. Within minutes of meeting the young furry lady, he vanished! We looked everywhere! We called his name. The entire neighbourhood looked for him. The newspaper announcements and the flyer posting did not help. We were devastated!

Soon after, one morning while consoling each other, Elizabeth mentioned to me that she always dreamed of having a Black Panther or a blue eye Siamese. Now it made sense her love for Mitzu, the little black cat. Quickly, I did some research and that very day, via media, we found a beautiful four month old female Siamese. We brought her home and Elizabeth named her, Mitzy.

Regardless, for me the pain of losing Mitzu had just begun. A mix feeling of obsession and depression was controlling my behaviour. I could not stop looking for him. To me he was like a child. I missed him! Probably because I was the one taking care of him when Elizabeth wasn't there. He loved hiding behind the corners and jumping to scare me, like a child.

I recall that The Princess of Wales, Diana, had died in Paris and I stayed up all night watching the news. By now, my pain had skyrocketed! I felt wave after wave of a very strange painful energy travelling through my body. Like me, the entire world was engaged in common grieving. Man and women were crying everywhere, more so the ones that felt betrayed by life, stuck in inappropriate bondage. To stay alive could cost some of us, our freedom. Anyone on Earth without love is suffering secretly, because love is the only divine at its best. Love is the most painful, yet the most wonderful gift given to humanity. Love can not be forced. It has to flow naturally. Humans who find love on Earth are the luckiest of all.

At the end of August, 1997, the television became a 24 hour funeral event. In a way it was therapeutic—on the other side, it forced me to stop and think how we can love so diversified and to such a degree. The beautiful images of Diana and her children were everywhere. I could clearly see half of humanity (psychologically) in Diana's shoes. How lucky for those who had love. How sad for those like me, who had never experienced true love. So, I sit there like the rest of the world caught in the clutches of CNN, CBC and BBC, reflecting and mourning my life.

Suddenly, a phone call from a lady who thought that our Mitzu has been taken to the animal shelter. I drove there as quickly as I could. Disappointment followed, and lots of extra tears. They brought in a dehydrated black kitten without a collar, and it was not Mitzu. So sick was the poor kitten that they put him to sleep.

While there, crying, another very sick kitten arrived. This one black and white without a tail. To end my tears a shelter employee, creatively, asked me to hold the kitten in my arms. They had just find him in a ravine, dirty, hungry, and with very bad breath from being sick. This cute kitty hugged me like a child, meowing softly in my ear, trying to eat my earlobe. He put his head on my shoulder like a baby. Without thinking twice, within minutes I adopted him and he came home with me, immediately. It was estimated that he also was four months old, just like Mitzy. When I named him Lelu, he said, "Meow," in approval.

Once home, I feed him. I give him a bath. I dried him in a towel. Then, I put him on antibiotics to fight the cold he couth in that ravine. Even his beautiful eyes were dripping badly, but I cured him. Regardless of the sickness, my Lelu was a happy boy. So very cute ... that I could not stop admiring his unique look. "He looks like a baby goat. He looks like a rabbit." I kept debating. Miraculously, all of a sudden I become happier around this fluffy bundle of love.

Soon, Lelu became healthy. He also become friends with Mitzy. Happiness was in the air. Because of the love that these two kitties brought us, Elizabeth and I were in heavens. Even better, Lelu and Mitzy started to eat with great appetite, played a lot and slept like little angels. On the other note, we become very productive. We had love in the house! I have to admit that without Elizabeth's original initiation to have Mitzu, and then Mitzy, I would have never gone to the shelter and meet Lelu. Without the Diana phenomena I would have not stoped to search my soul so deeply for the hope and love I needed. I have to thank God for the eye opening. No one lives or dies in vain. We all continuously change ourselves and the world around us. Our pets and all nature are part of "WE" the intelligent life on Earth. Love is the commander in chief.

THE PHOTOGRAPHED STORY

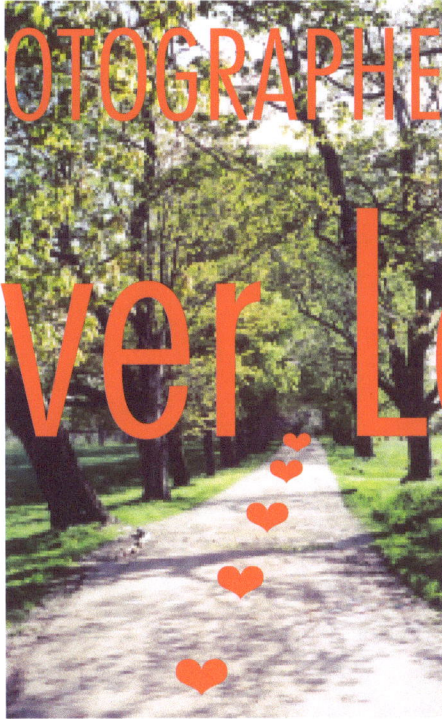

Forever Loved

LELU AND MITZY WERE BORN IN APRIL 1997 IN CANADA.
WE ADOPTED THEM AT THE END OF AUGUST THE SAME YEAR. SOON, THEY FELL IN LOVE ...

THEIR LOVE STORY
IS THE MOST BEAUTIFUL KITTY LOVE STORY I HAVE EVER KNOWN

MITZY

LELU

Mitzy was shy ... She was also confused. When I arrived home with Lelu and I introduced him to her, she meowed until she lost her voice. She has never seen a cat without a tail or a cat with yellow eyes. He was alien to her.

Lelu was also shy ... But he was humbled! Instantly, he made himself at home.

He was surprised to see Mitzy's tail, her blue eyes, and to hear her meow so loud. But he was also fascinated with her moves. "Gosh, she's elegant. I'll court her."

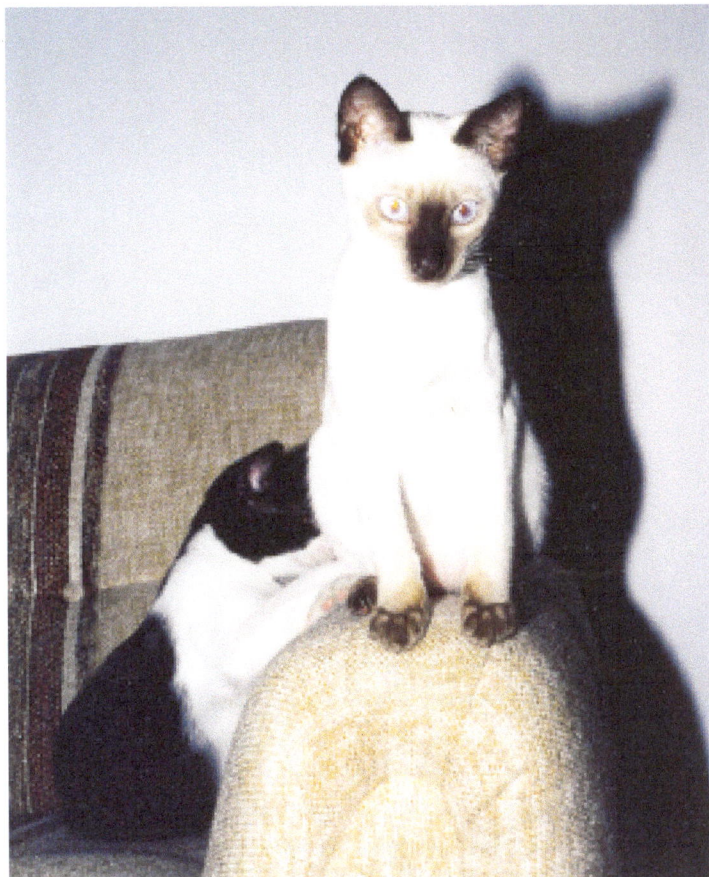

Lelu, "Let me see your tail."

Mitsy, "OK, but do not pull it."

Mitzy would ask for toys.
Lelu would just listen.
Together they would play so beautifully.

Mitzy discovered that Lelu loved playing with her tail.
She would stay there teasing him until he would get tired.

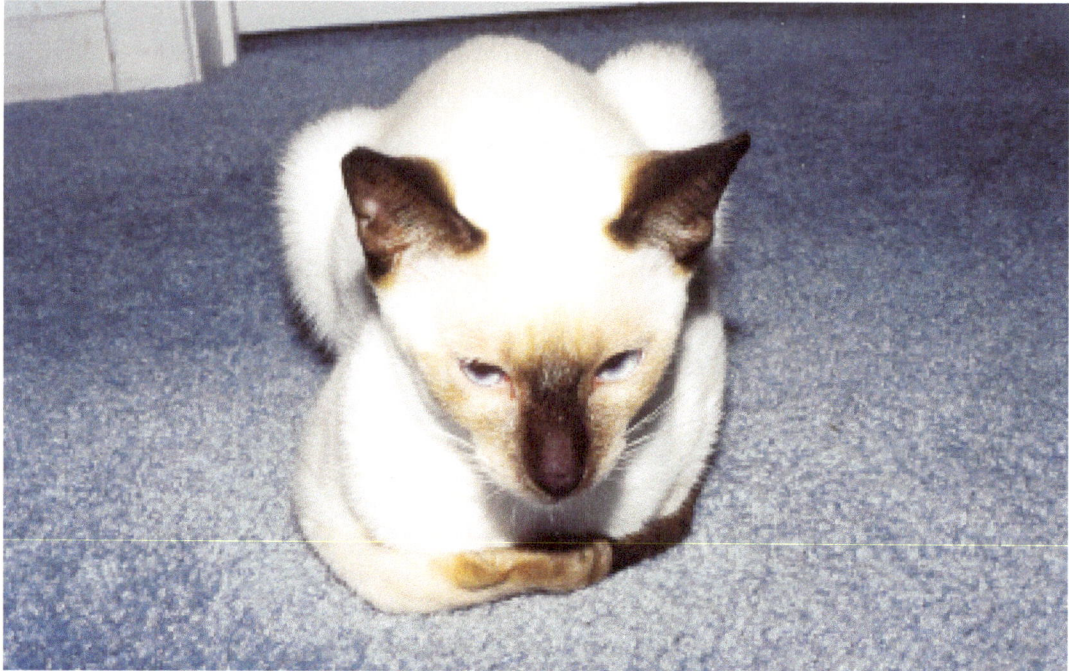

Young Mitzy would relax her way.
Lelu, like a kid, would relax his way.

Lelu and Mitzy playing silly at thanksgiving.

They were still babies, approximately six months old.

Right: When I saw Lelu relaxing in this position, I simply could not believe it.

Look at his face!

I never won a staring contest with Lelu. He had the capacity to stare without a blink, intimidating anyone.

Many people told me that Lelu looks human.

Mitzy, "I love roses ..."

Lelu, "The National Geographic stimulates me!"

Above: Mitzy loved leading the game. Lelu loved playing clown.

Below: Lelu loved wrestling. Mitzy loved Jiu-Jitsu. They were professional.

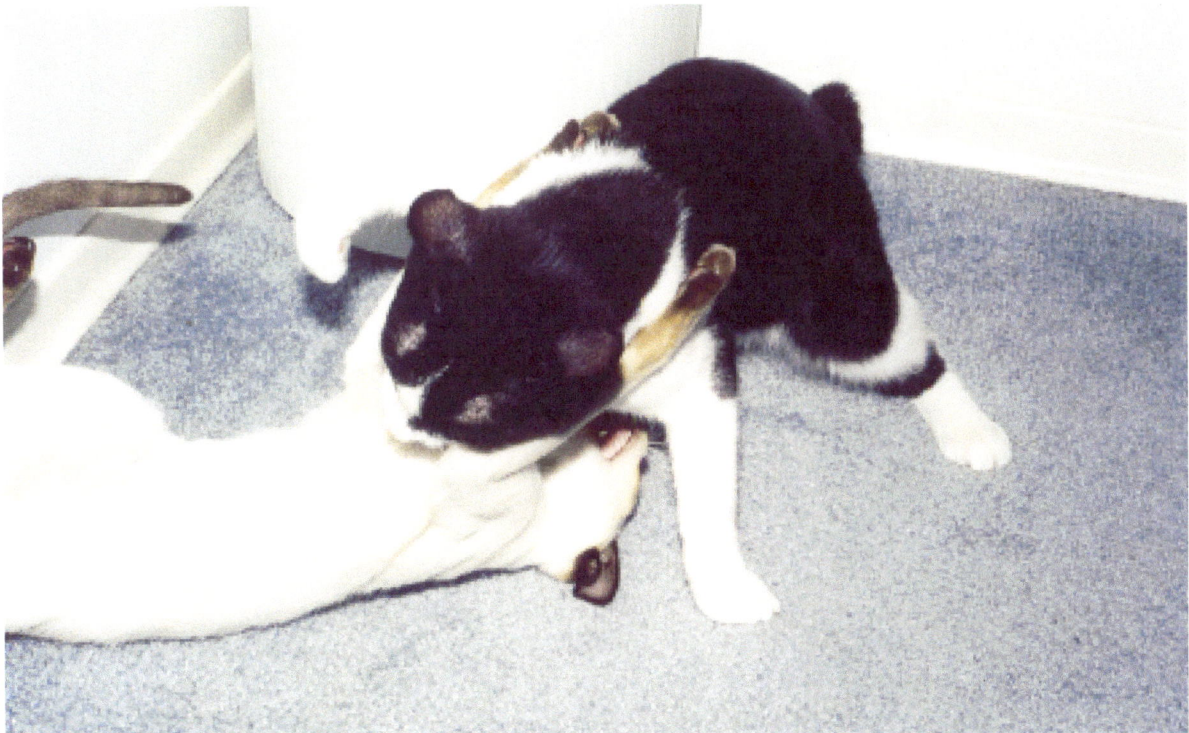

Lelu and Mitzy knew that practice makes it better.

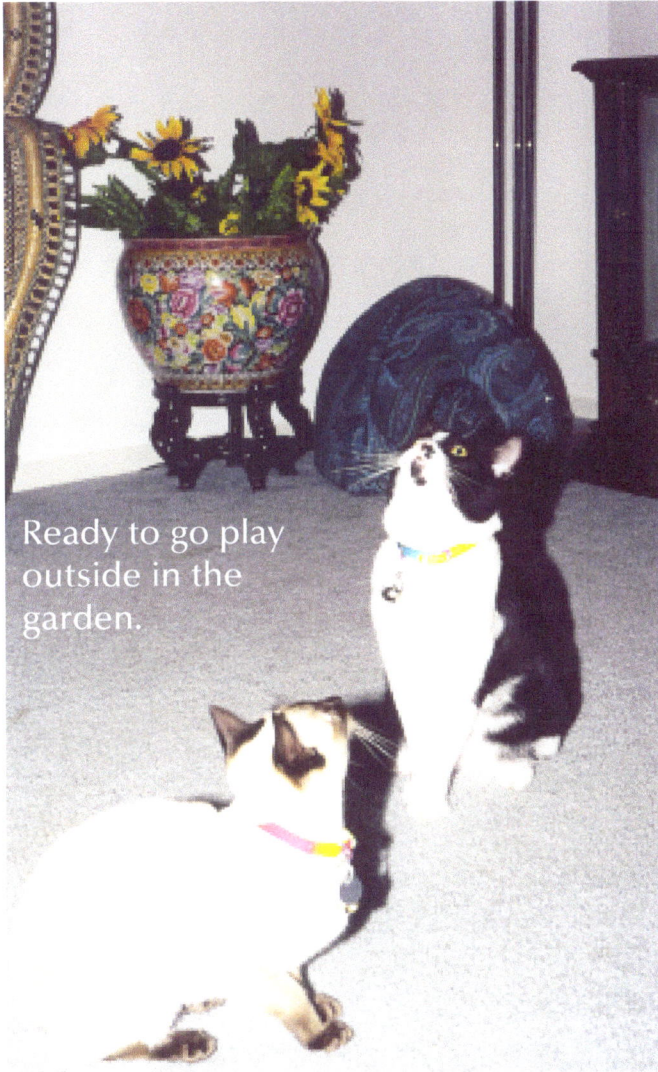

Ready to go play outside in the garden.

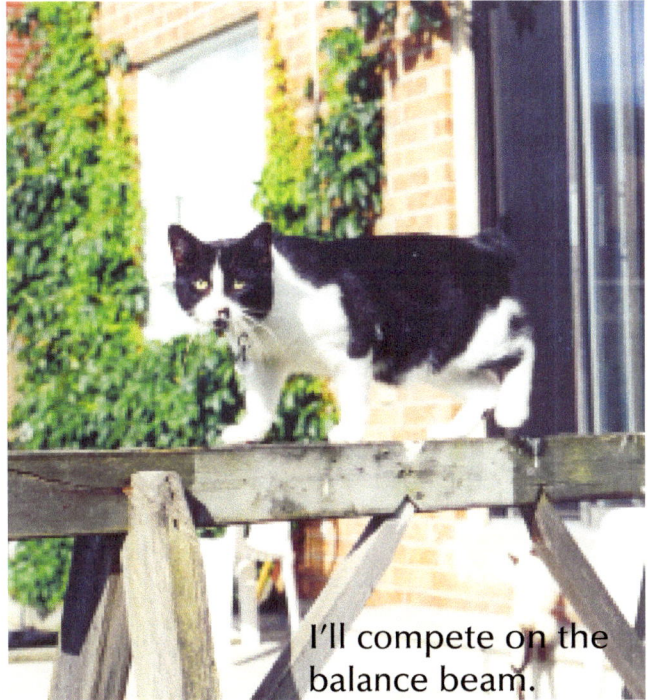

I'll compete on the balance beam.

Preparing for the olympics.

Lelu as a teenager, tranquily monitoring the outside activities.

Lelu young and beautiful. Very healthy. Very happy. Sweet and peaceful. Curiously watching TV like a human.

Below: Sleeping like a child ...

Above: Lelu, "Be careful darling."

Above: Lelu french-grooming Mitzy on the back of her head.

Below: They were so young, yet so smartly in love. Fidelity all the way. Lelu's timidity and Mitzy's tranquility are clearly visible from their facial expressions.

Left: Mitzy, "Whoever invented this screen is guilty of ruining my nail."

Lelu, "Do not worry, my love. I am a man. I will get to the bottom of this. There should be a way to open this and get out in the garden."

Lelu, very sleepy ...

Lelu, "Let me lean my head on your abdomen.

Oh, I'm so in love ..."

Mitzy showing her super-manicure. She loved a good game.

Mitzy on the leash, as a temporary precaution until she learned to stay in her safe garden. She scared us terribly when, unaware, she attempted to jump over the fence into a neighbours garden where two large dogs were waiting to devour her.

Below, Lelu protecting the black currant bushes, the mint and the catnip.

Lelu and Mitzy enjoying the indoor.

We provided them with lots of opportunity to admire the outdoor activities and nature via uncovered windows.

Squirrels and birds would nest outside the windows some years. Lelu and Mitzy loved the small traffic especially when home alone. When we were home, they were in the garden for hours at a time.

For this special family I provided a basket, I put the eggs in there and the mother was so happy that she raised two sets of children in one summer. If she could only speak ...

Lelu and Mitzy would never attack the birds. They just watch them with curiosity.

Lelu loved the basket.

Mitzy loved the sun.

Relaxing in the shade.

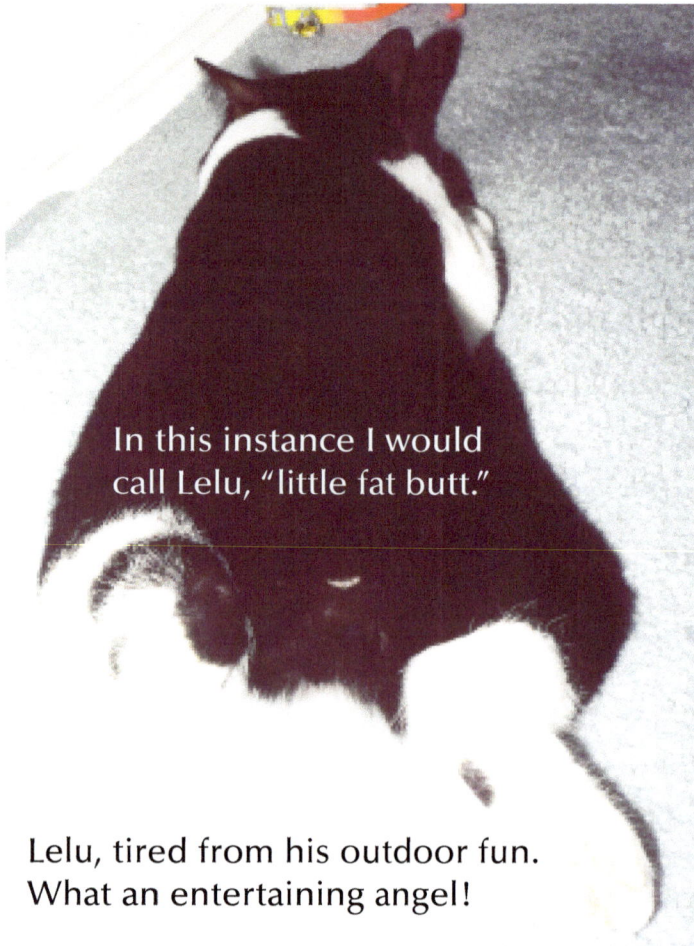

In this instance I would call Lelu, "little fat butt."

Lelu, tired from his outdoor fun. What an entertaining angel!

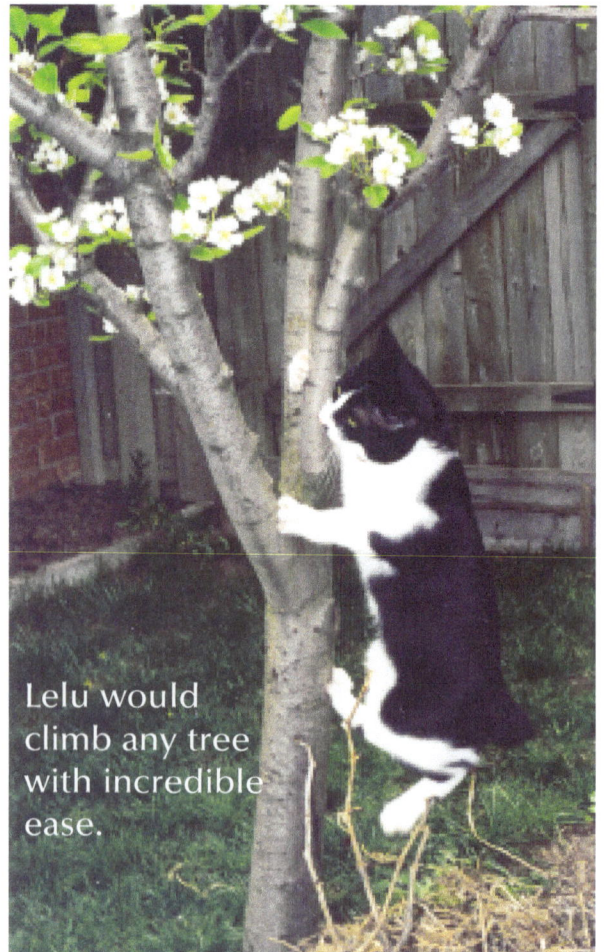

Lelu would climb any tree with incredible ease.

Mitzy off the leash for good. She never again gave us any emotions. She learned to enjoy her garden and watch the adventurous Lelu playing clown.

Indoors, Mitzy and Lelu had a kitty house, toys, brushes, and complete freedom.

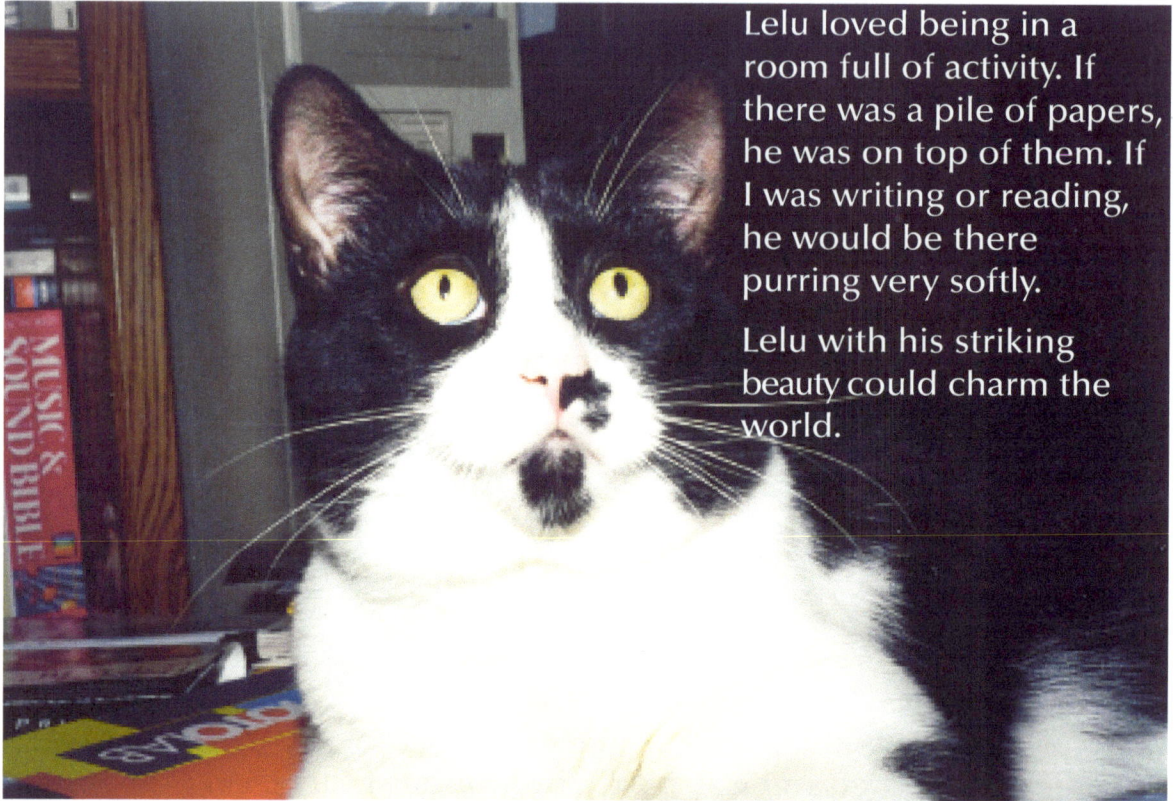

Lelu loved being in a room full of activity. If there was a pile of papers, he was on top of them. If I was writing or reading, he would be there purring very softly.

Lelu with his striking beauty could charm the world.

The house was covered in green. It was a splendour—for birds, bees, butterflies, other insects, squirrels, humans, and for Lelu.

Many times I sat there with Lelu and Mitzy—writing poetry.

Often, Lelu would just stay in front of an open window, tranquil.

Lelu loved food so much so that he grew very big. He became very solid and strong—17 lbs. He ate Fancy Feast as wet food, IAMS and Whiskas as dry food. He drank water like a human, with his paw, always. Within a few years, Lelu became a glorious Manx with a very shiny coat, as he is shown in the picture below. And yes, he would jump very, very high.

Lelu loved very much relaxing on his back.

Mitzy did find plenty of tranquility in the garden or even on the shelf in the basement beside the food supplies. She also ate well and developed into a glorious young lady who always showed manners other cats could only dream of. To let her know that I appreciate elegance, I often called her, "Your Majesty ..." and bowed to her. When indoors, I always took the collar off Lelu and Mitzy to let them feel free.

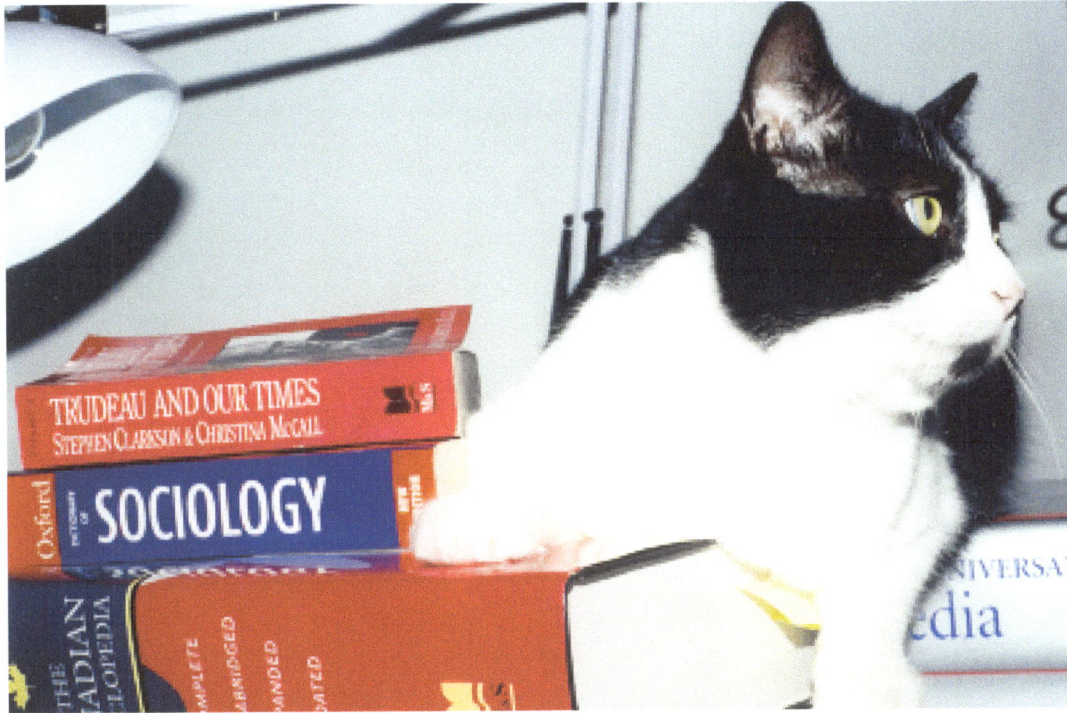

I love books and Lelu knew it. He was always on top of them and he was incredibly intelligent. I do believe that many animals are very, very smart. Lelu felt like a human. He just knew everything. He even imitated barking dogs. He was also my clock. With incredible precision, five minutes before the alarm would go off, he would come on the side of my bed, he would stand up and meow softly or touched me.

Left: Lelu, "Mommy, what are we? Conservative or Liberal?"

Mommy, "We are modern believers in human rights and kitty rights. On Parliament Hill in Ottawa there is already a cat colony making buzz. Kitty politicians."

Lelu, "Do those cats need a Prime Minister? I know I would be good. I'm a modern Manx!"

Christmas was incredible fun. Now that I look back, I realize that I let Lelu and Mitzy even get on the table. But they never did it when we were eating, only to pose for some special occasion. I think that they knew the difference. As cards would arrive from all over the place, Lelu would nest right between them, like in this picture.

Mitzy was after tiny toys. She was also very daring and forever curious. Unlike Lelu, this tiny Siamese was not afraid of many things. If she heard some knocking, she would come running to see what was going on. Often she was between hammers and nails, observing how things are being assembled.

But, for some reason, both Lelu and Mitzy were very afraid of lightning and thunder. They would come running and hide behind me or somewhere in a closet, together. I would always reassure them that they were safe. "Lelu, Mitzy, it is OK babies, it is Ok ... Do not be afraid. Mommy is here."

I like you ...

Lelu would climb up the Christmas tree every single year. For him it was incredible fun. Mitzy would just seat beside and watch. She rarely had the opportunity to do the same. I do believe that Lelu must have informed her from early on that the tree was his. Not only once did the tree flip over with Lelu in it.

Lelu, "This toy is mine."

Mitzy, "I do not have to climb a tree in order to make myself visible ..."

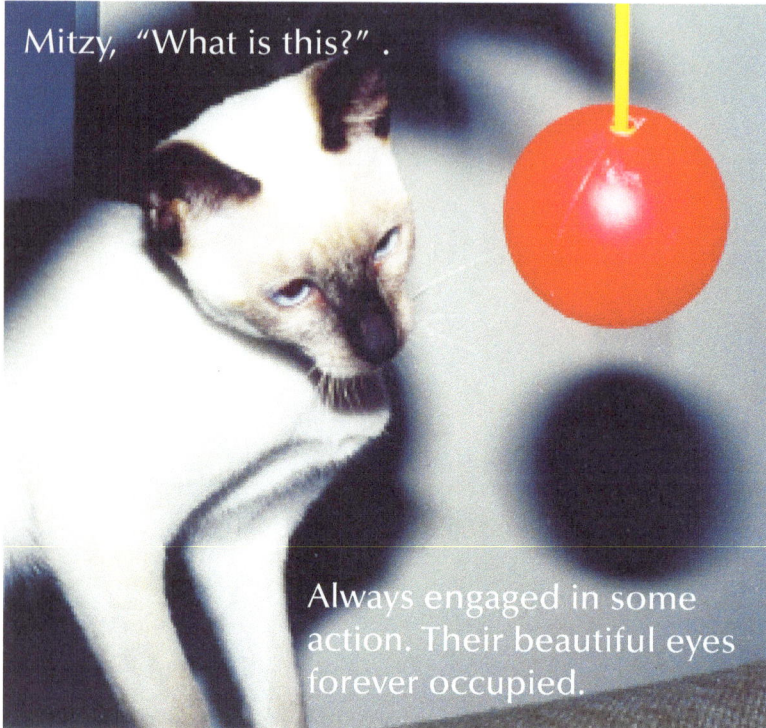

Mitzy, "What is this?" .

Always engaged in some action. Their beautiful eyes forever occupied.

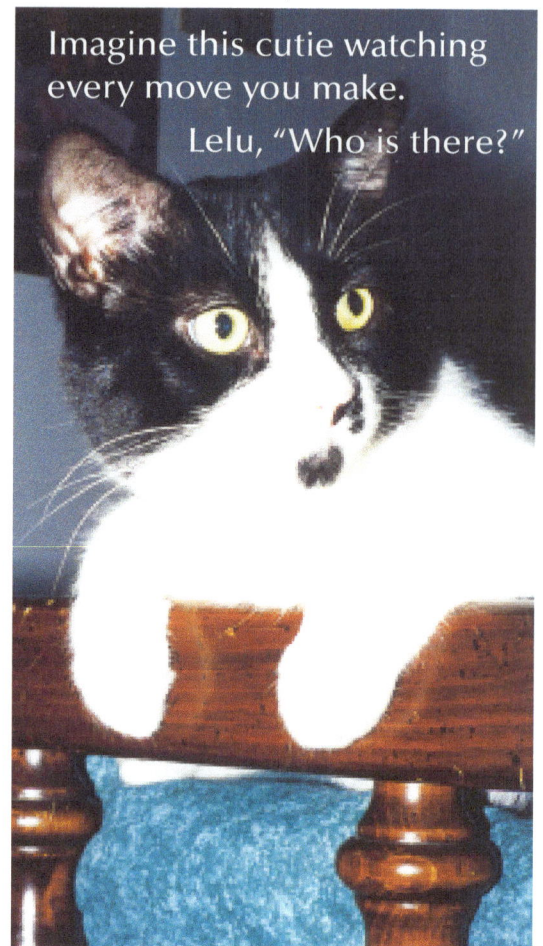

Imagine this cutie watching every move you make.

Lelu, "Who is there?"

Below: Lelu was a bit uncomfortable when one year old Cookie, a neighbour's male cat, would come to our door to peak in. Soon after this picture was taken Cookie drowned in another neighbour's swimming pool. He had been declawed and when he slid in, he could not get out. Our neighbour, Maria, was absolutely devastated. She cried inconsolably.

Cookie

Lelu

Above: One of Lelu's peek-a-boo moments. He was all play. He would emerge from the least expected places and often scared me.

Below: Lelu lived between books, no wonder he was so smart.

Lelu and Mitzy in their teens.

Mitzy would sleep on top of my computer.

Lelu opted for my bed, his bed, or the top of my printer.

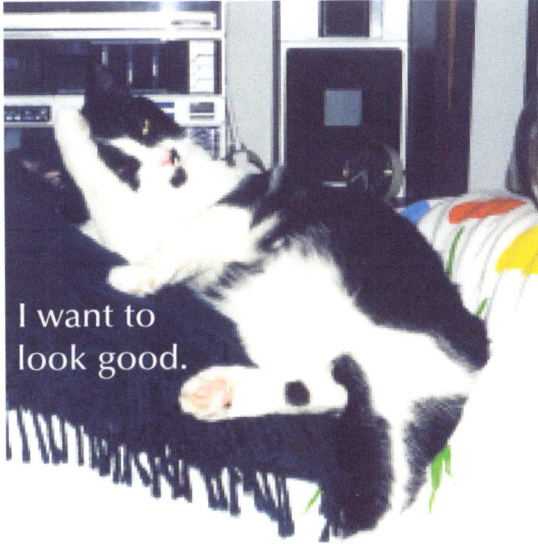

I want to
look good.

Uh, this is good

This bed feels
like heavens.

Lelu eating his favourite meat. He also consumed milk until he was one and a half year old, then suddenly stopped. Within two years, he grew so big that I had to purchase him a dog size bed. That's where he could spread comfortably. The picture on the left shows how much he loved it.

Below, Lelu on my IBM, yawning.

Lelu, "Mommy! I'm sleepy ..."

Mommy, "I see. Get off the IBM and go to bed."

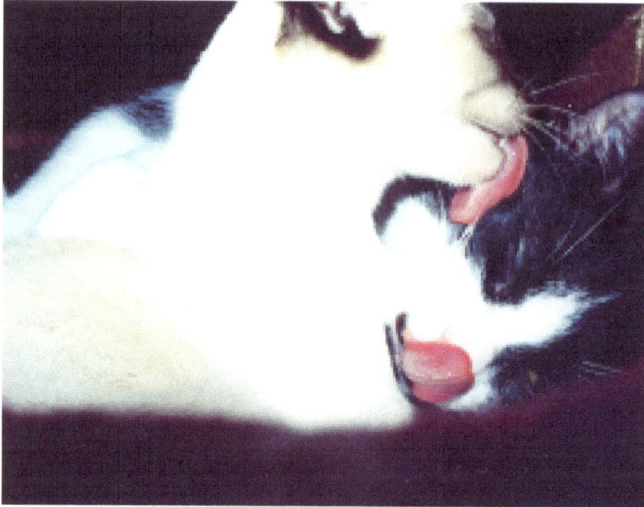

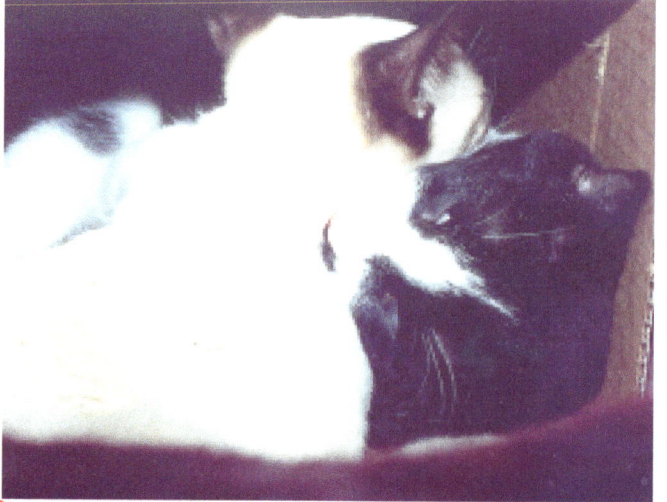

Lelu and Mitzy in 2003. All they needed was a box and their enormous love.

LELU AND MITZY

ADULTS

Lelu played ball a lot and was very good at it. I often played with him.

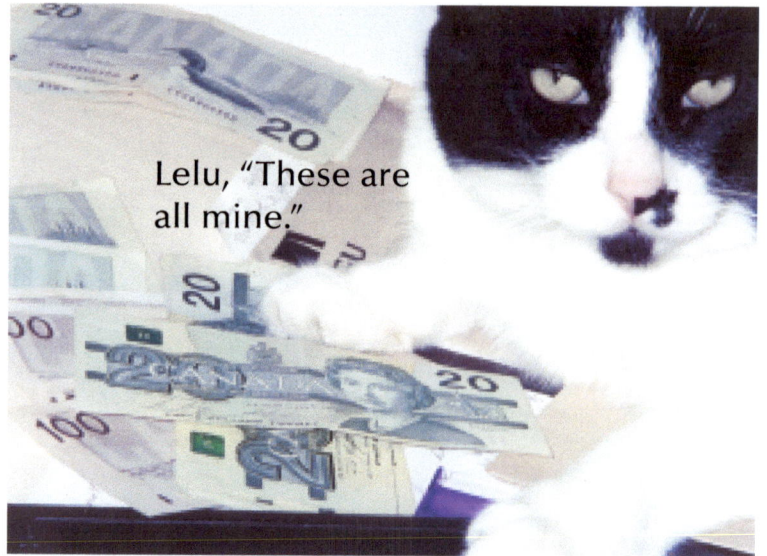

Lelu, "These are all mine."

Top right: Lelu, "I worked hard for the money and I am going to have a good life."

Top Left: Lelu, "This house was expensive, but I am a special boy and I deserve the gift."

Below: On his favourite IKEA chair.

Sweet life ...
Sweet dreams ...

The aging process did not affect much Lelu and Mitzy.

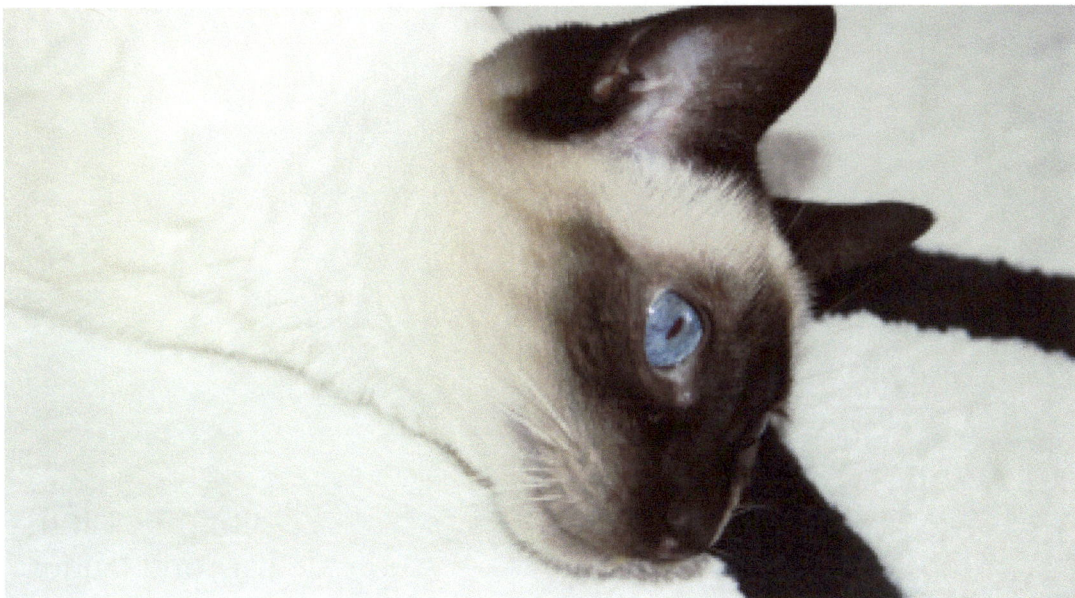

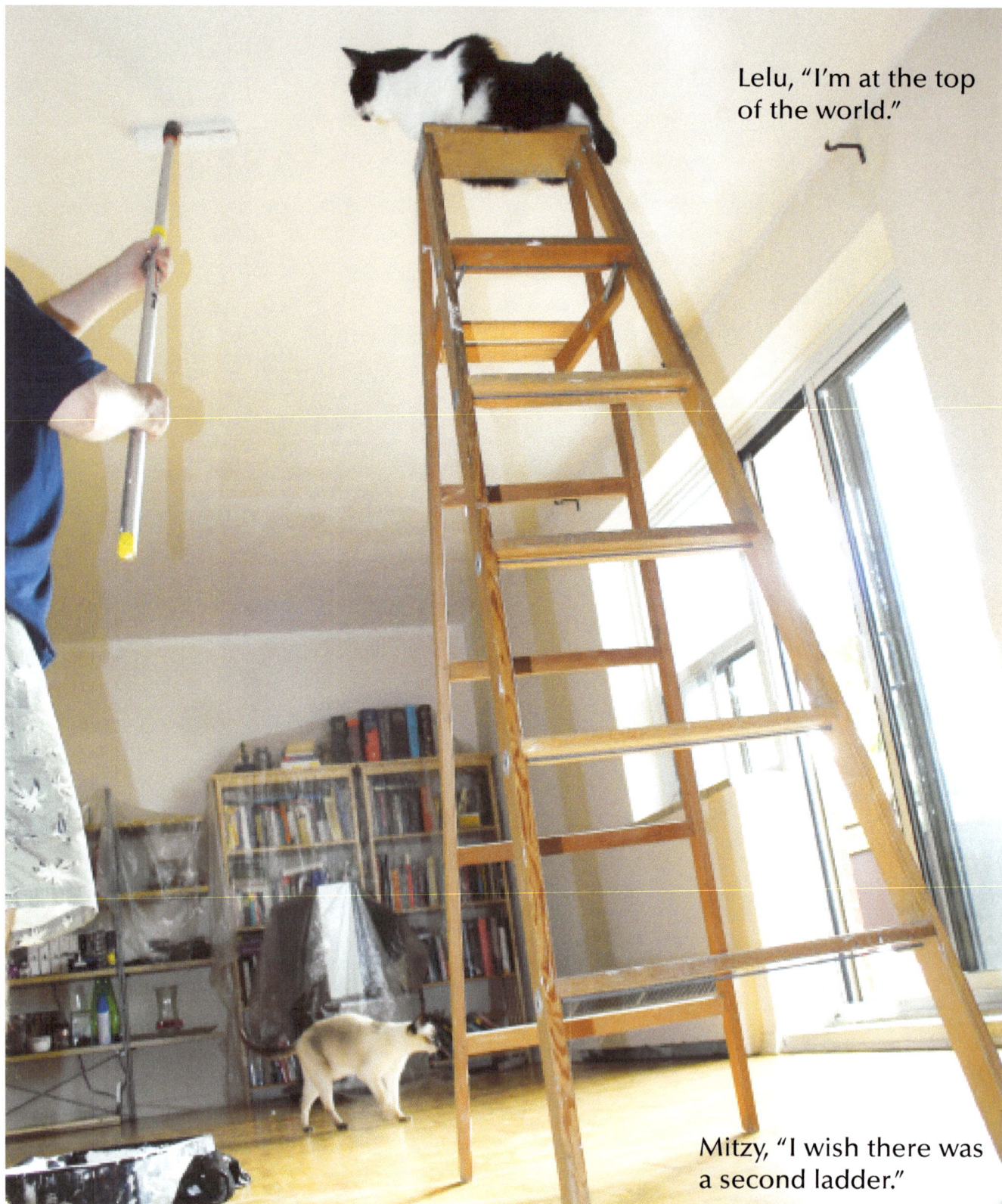

Lelu, "I'm at the top of the world."

Mitzy, "I wish there was a second ladder."

Lelu would negotiate for his right to stay up there longer.

For Lelu and Mitzy sleepover was a permanent right.

The touch of love ...

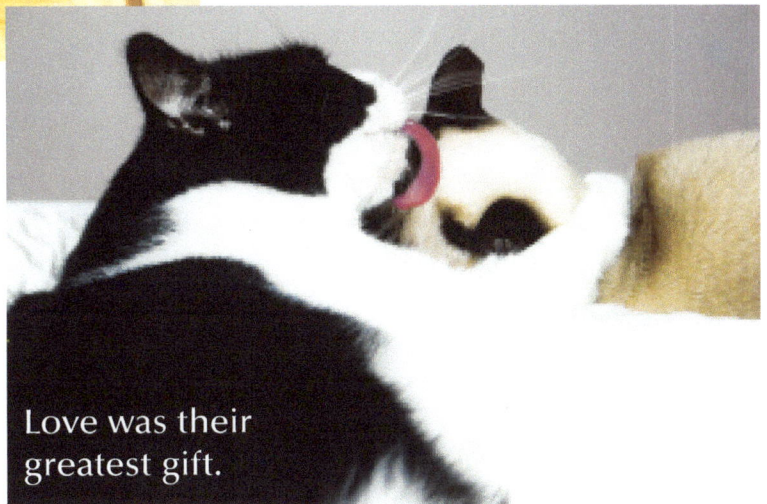

Love was their greatest gift.

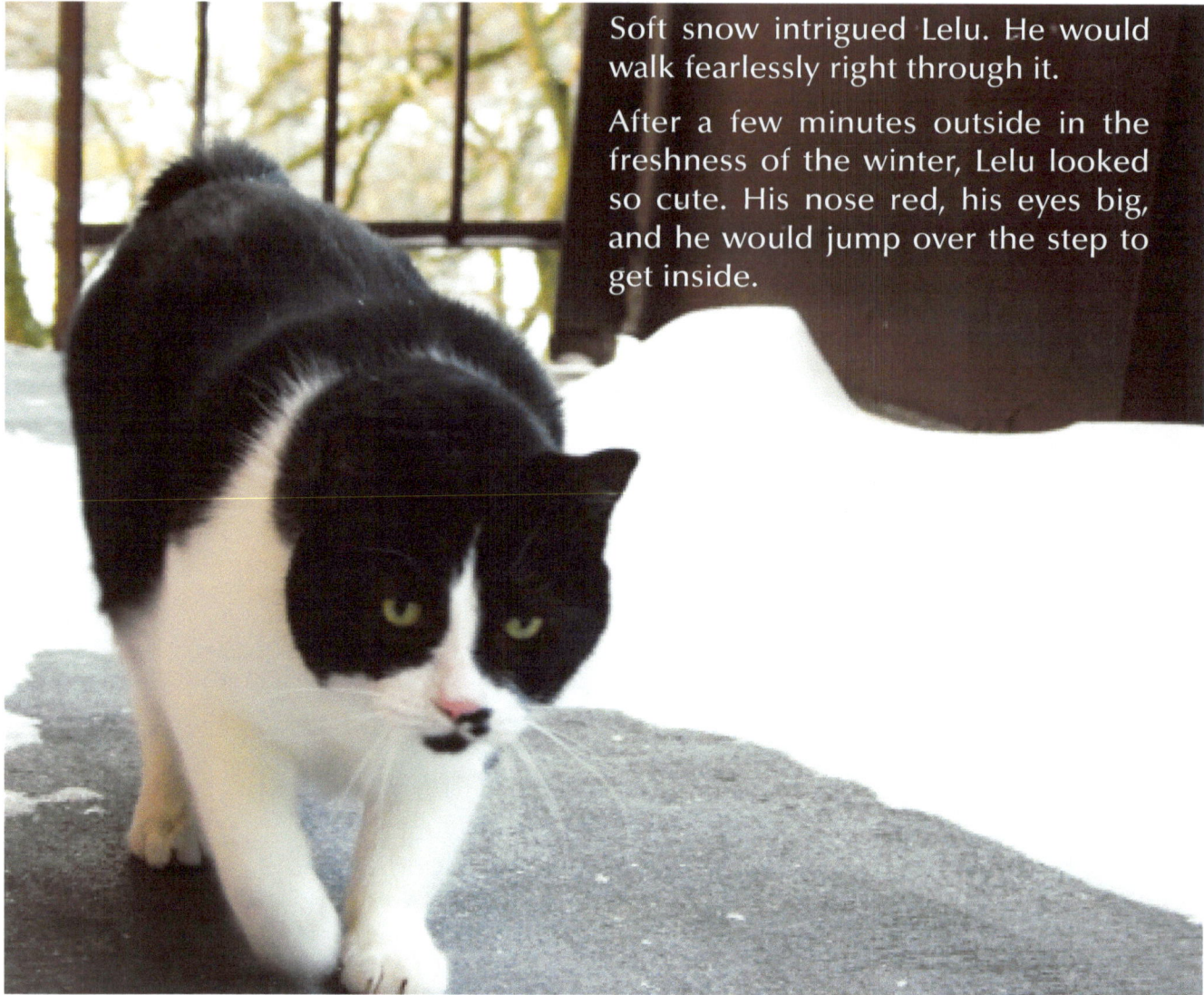

Soft snow intrigued Lelu. He would walk fearlessly right through it.

After a few minutes outside in the freshness of the winter, Lelu looked so cute. His nose red, his eyes big, and he would jump over the step to get inside.

Lelu, "What is there?"

Hoop!

For easy maintenance in their main area I did not keep carpets. I followed a reasonable routine and kept it clean at all times.

From time to time I would purchase new pillows and place them in baskets or decorated boxes.

Lelu and Mitzy had their soft beds separate from these extra places of comfort. Occasionally, they would trade places. A lot of commerce was going on.

Since they were six months old:

Lelu was neutered.

Mitzy was spayed.

We would vacuum daily everywhere in order to keep the house clean.

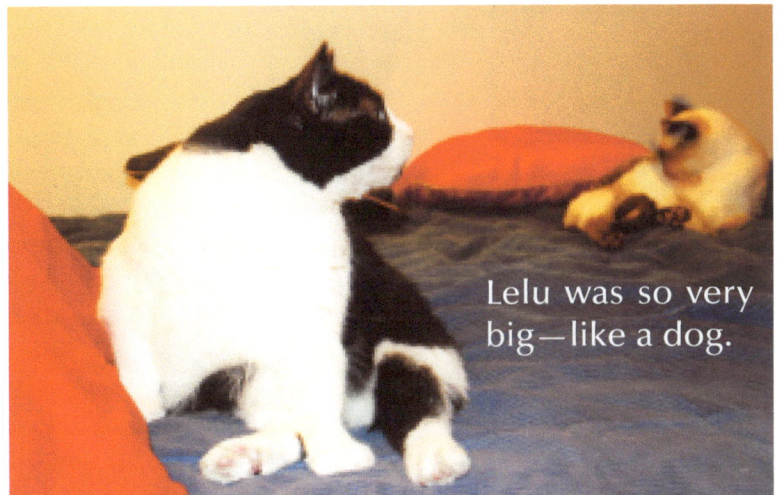

Lelu was so very big—like a dog.

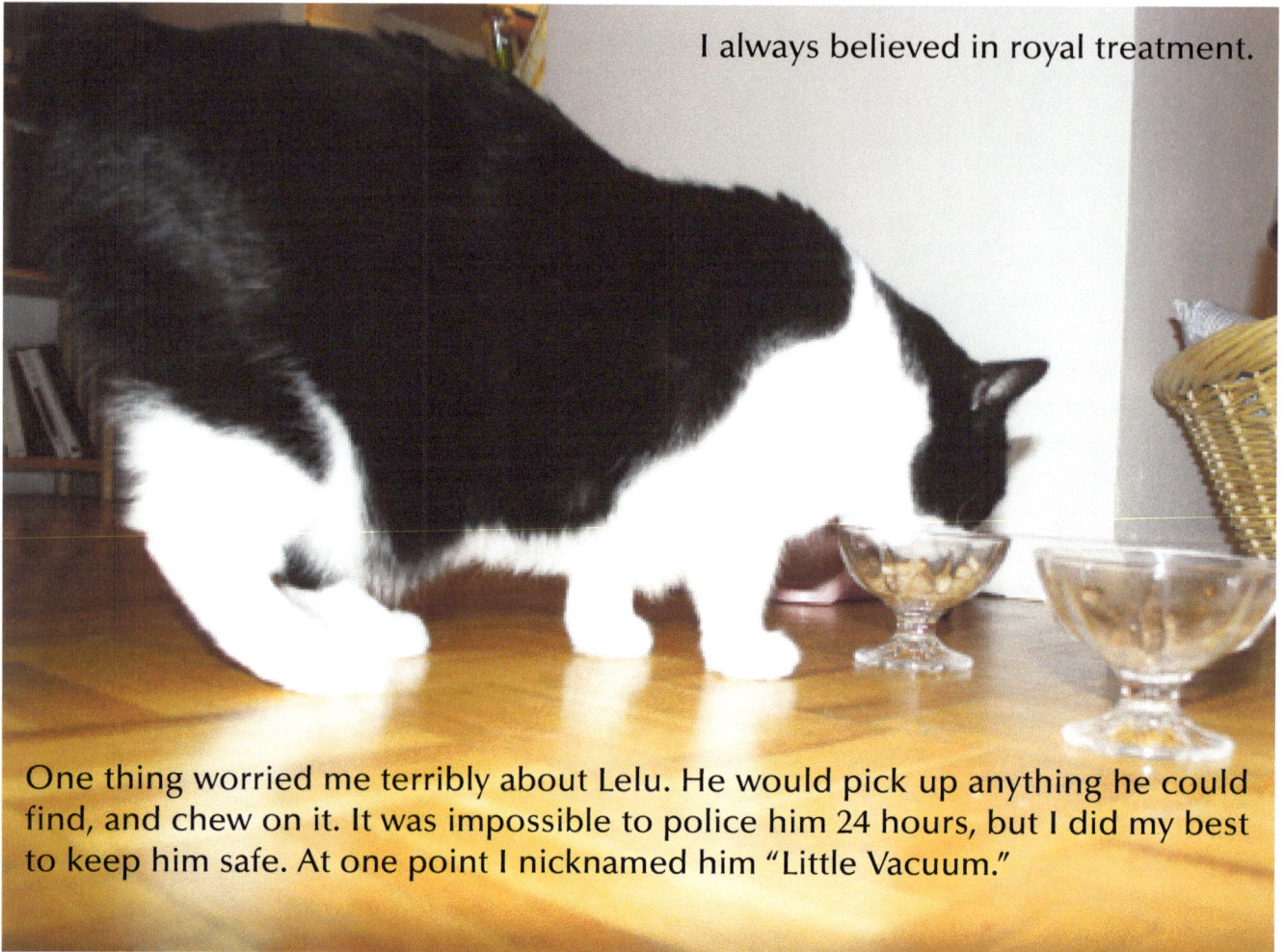

I always believed in royal treatment.

One thing worried me terribly about Lelu. He would pick up anything he could find, and chew on it. It was impossible to police him 24 hours, but I did my best to keep him safe. At one point I nicknamed him "Little Vacuum."

About the scratching post, what can I say? The IKEA wooden furniture was their favourite target. Lelu and Mitzy had their nails intact. No one could stop them from sharpening their manicure, but I did make sure that they stayed with four table legs and a bookshelf, leaving the rest of the furniture intact. They were free to walk, play and sleep anywhere they wanted in the house. We never close any door. But if they tried to scratch non-permissible items, I would spray some perfume on that item, and they never did it again. Cats do not like strong perfume. "Yuck!"

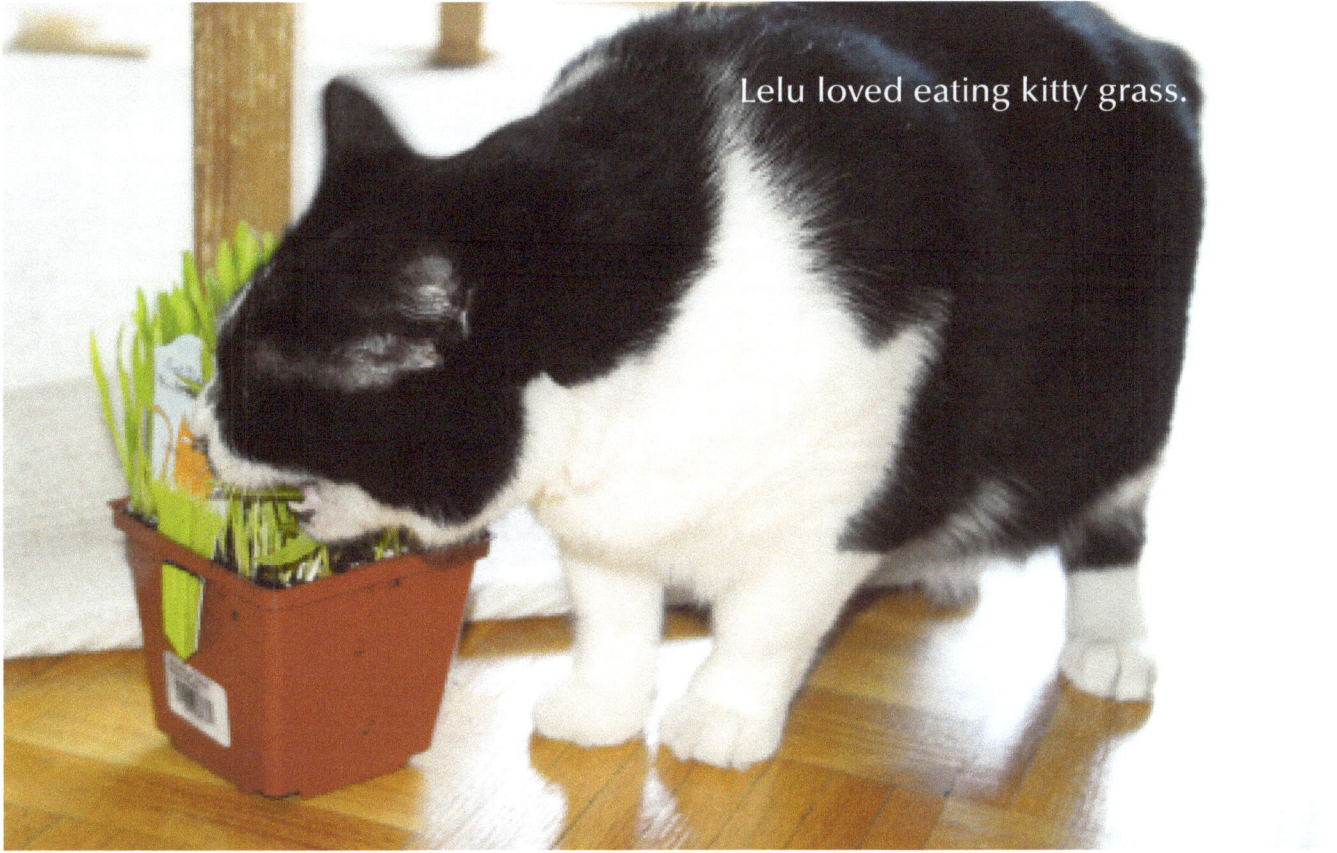

Lelu loved eating kitty grass.

Here, Lelu wrapped himself in curtains like a bride.

Lelu 's secondary bed.

Lelu knew that he was adored. I told him so every day of his life. He would rub his face in my palm and just dream.

If my hands were busy, then he would find my leg as a good replacement. The touch ... was very important.

Mitzy washing herself.

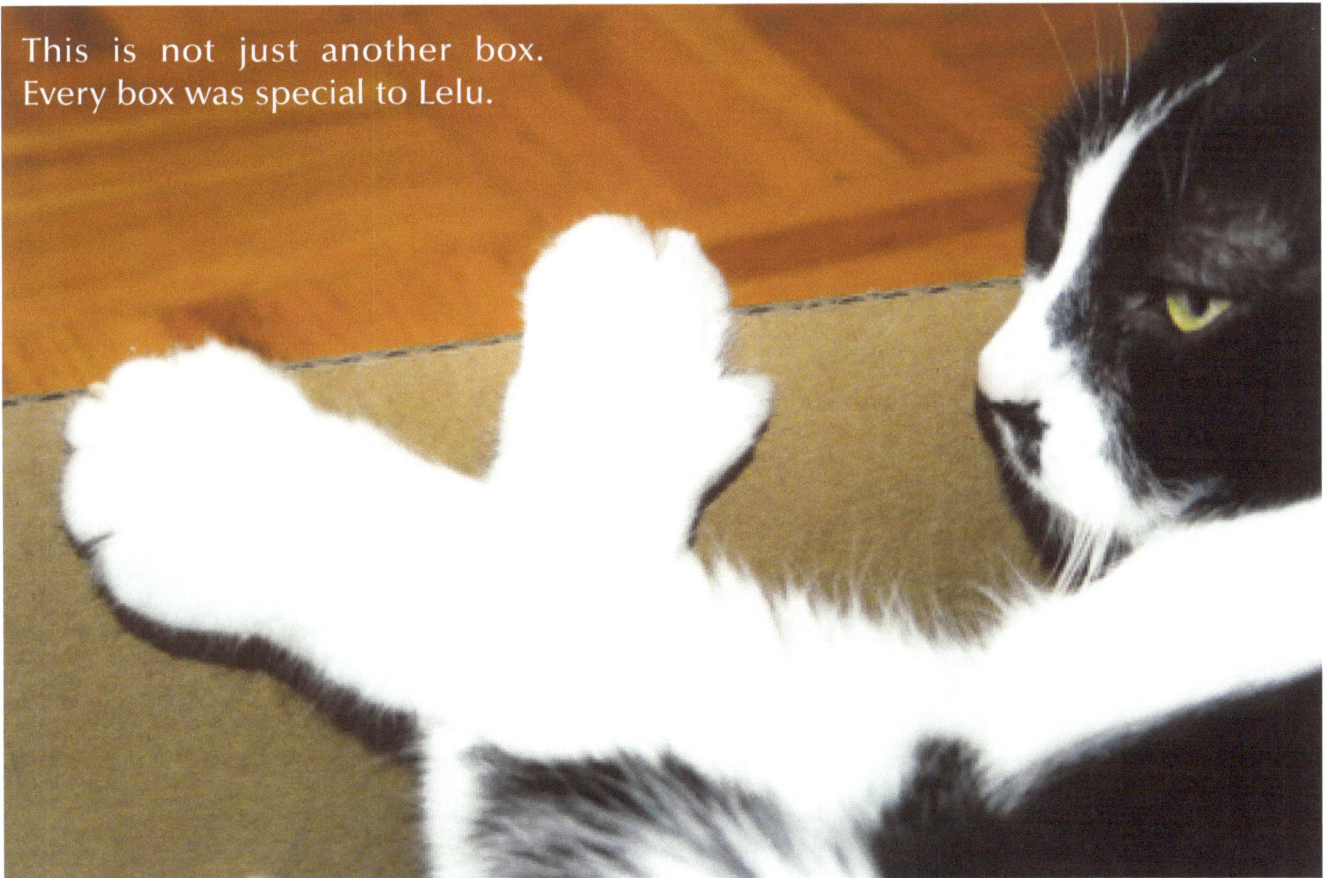

This is not just another box.
Every box was special to Lelu.

This image made me tranquil.

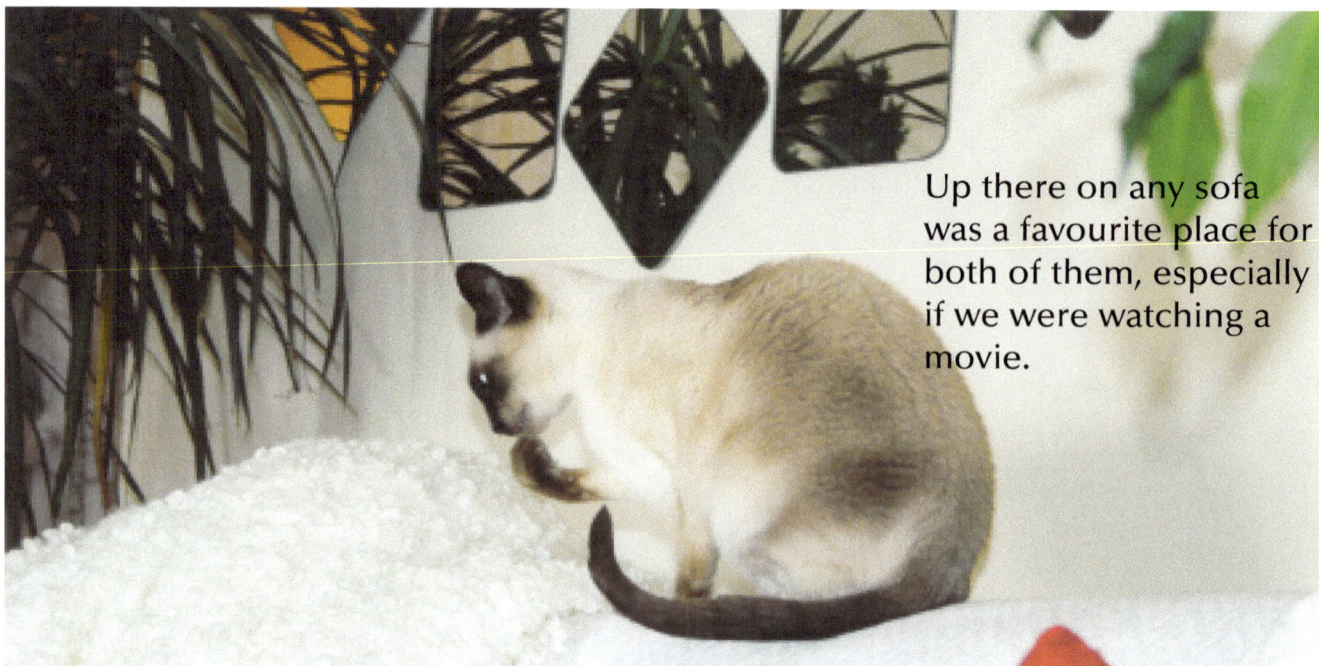

Up there on any sofa was a favourite place for both of them, especially if we were watching a movie.

Any place, any time, the display was the same. This glorious feline with his legs up, with just one nail securing the spread beneath, and as you see from his facial expression denoting, "Peace is good."

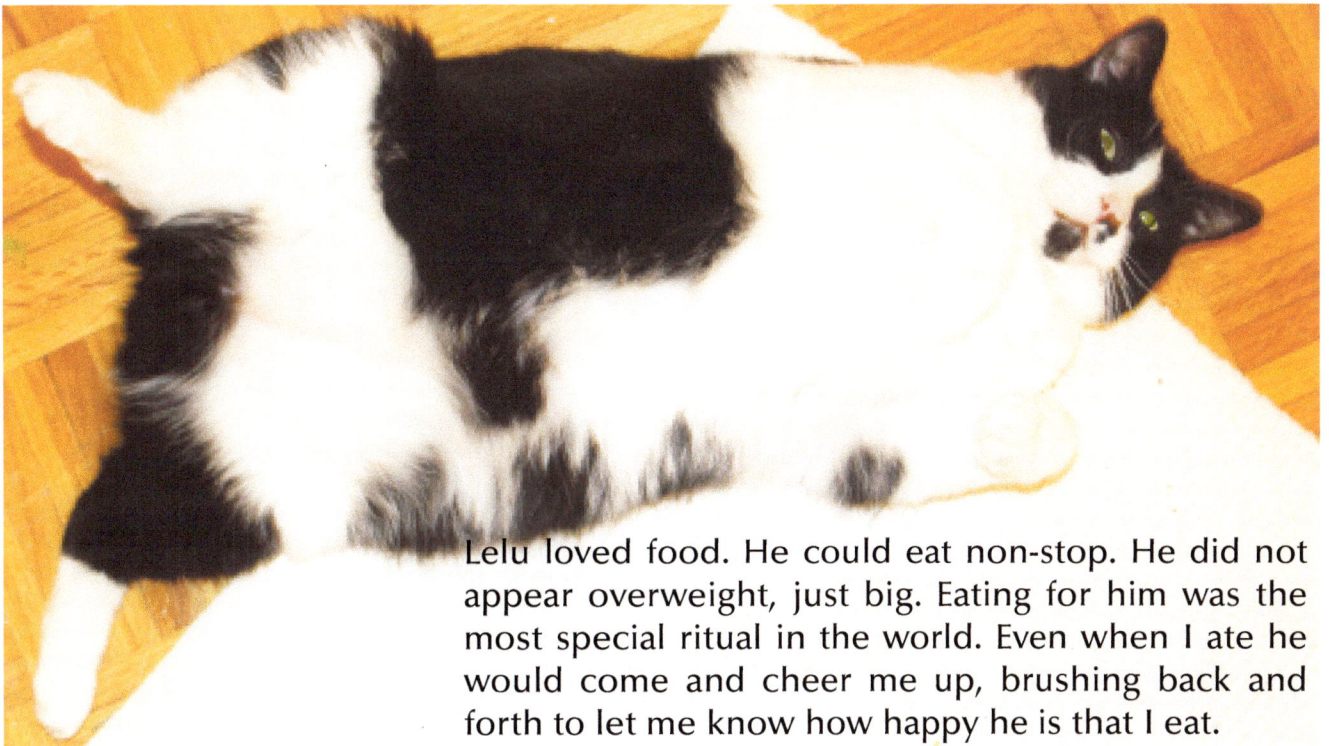

Lelu loved food. He could eat non-stop. He did not appear overweight, just big. Eating for him was the most special ritual in the world. Even when I ate he would come and cheer me up, brushing back and forth to let me know how happy he is that I eat.

Elizabeth surrounded by love ...

Lots of love ...
Babies & Cats.

Mitzy "Another baby?"
Lelu, "Let me see."

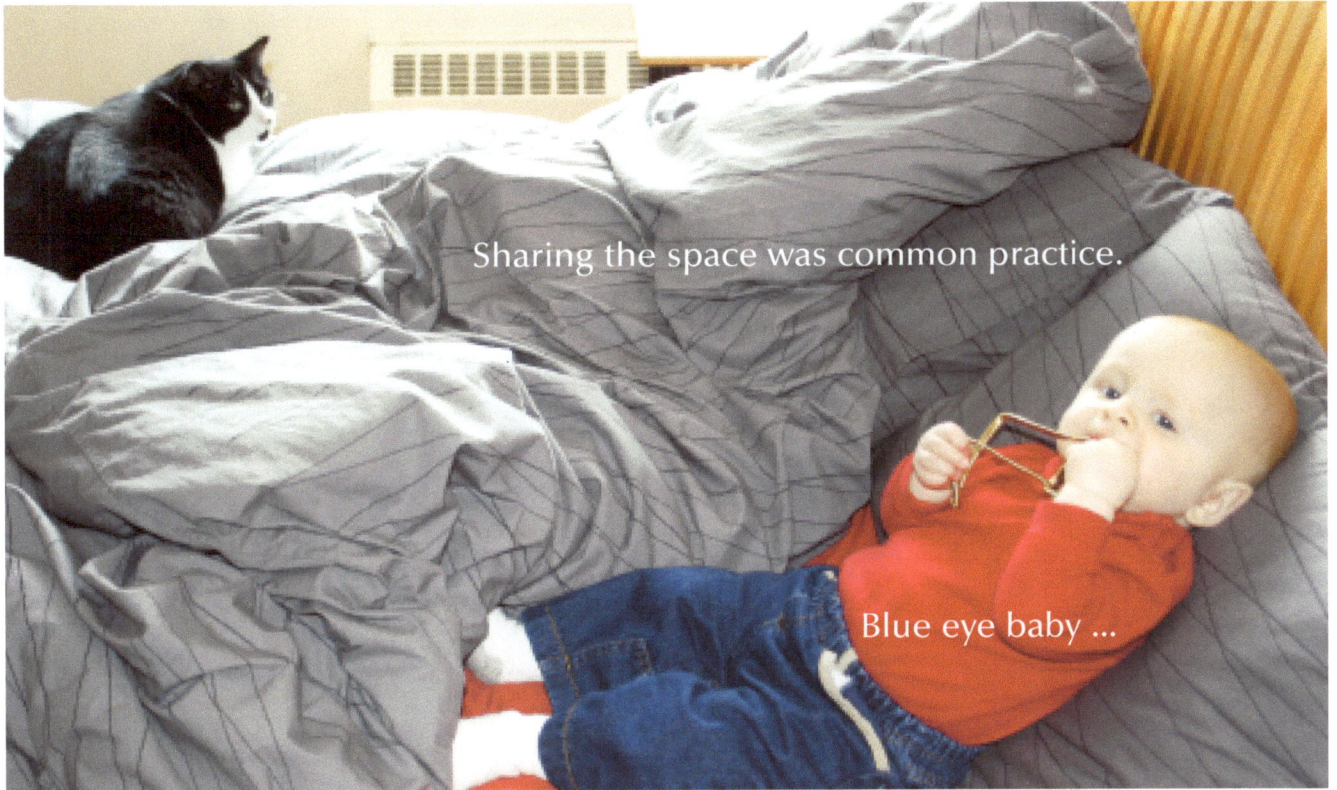

Sharing the space was common practice.

Blue eye baby ...

Blue eye cat ...

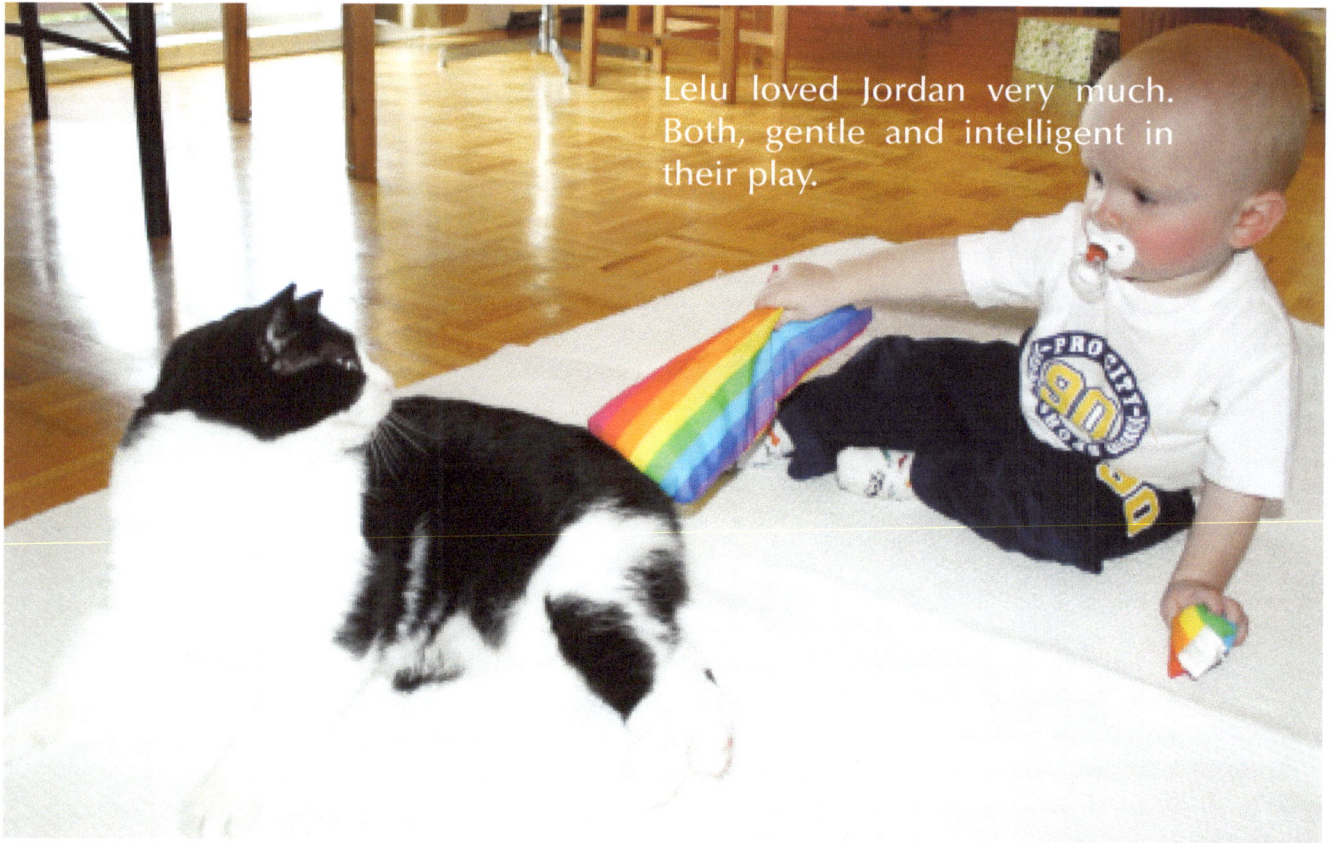

Lelu loved Jordan very much. Both, gentle and intelligent in their play.

Lelu to Jordan, "That wiener must be delicious!"

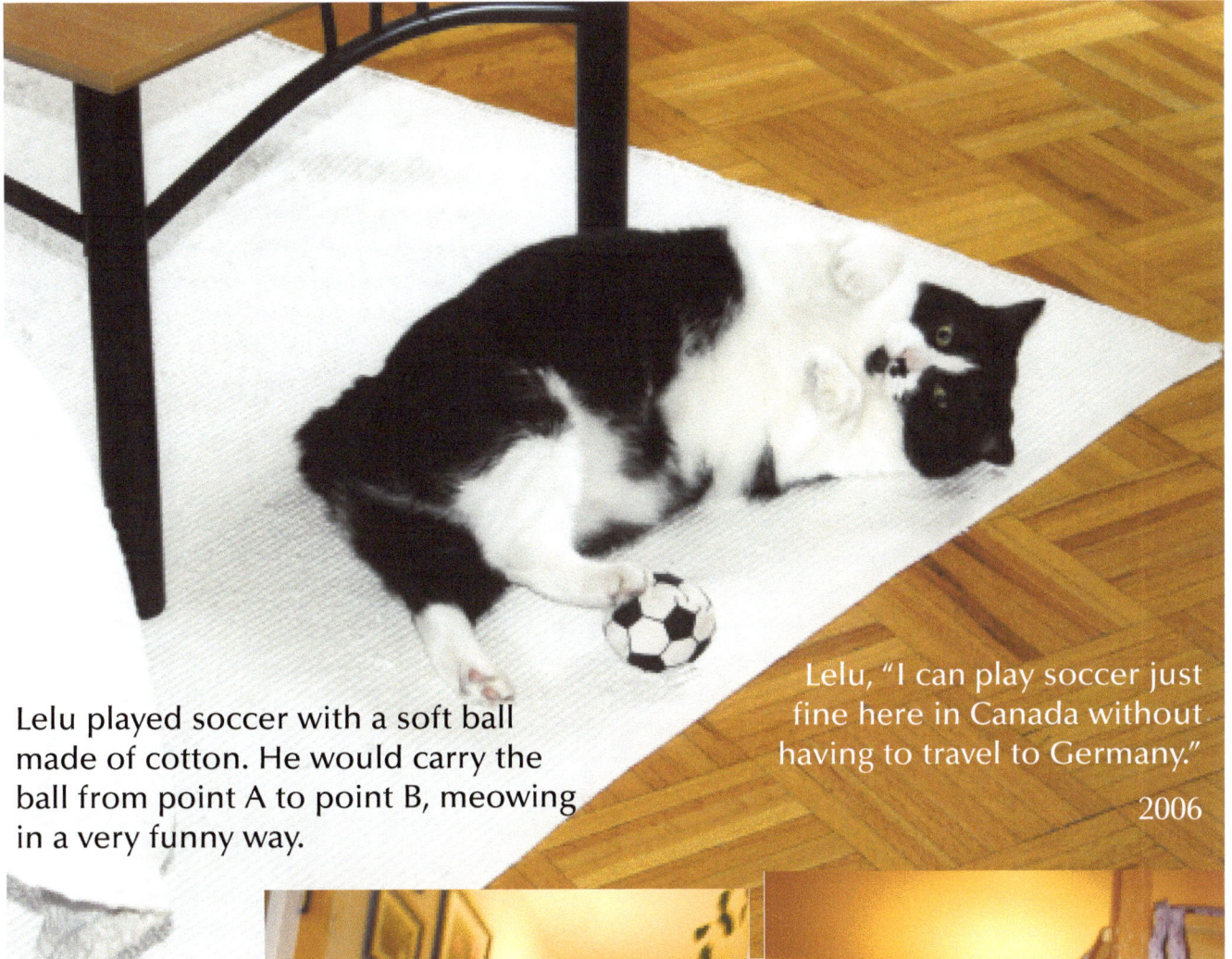

Lelu played soccer with a soft ball made of cotton. He would carry the ball from point A to point B, meowing in a very funny way.

Lelu, "I can play soccer just fine here in Canada without having to travel to Germany."

2006

Mitzy would court little Jordan for a few caresses here and there. She loved being followed.

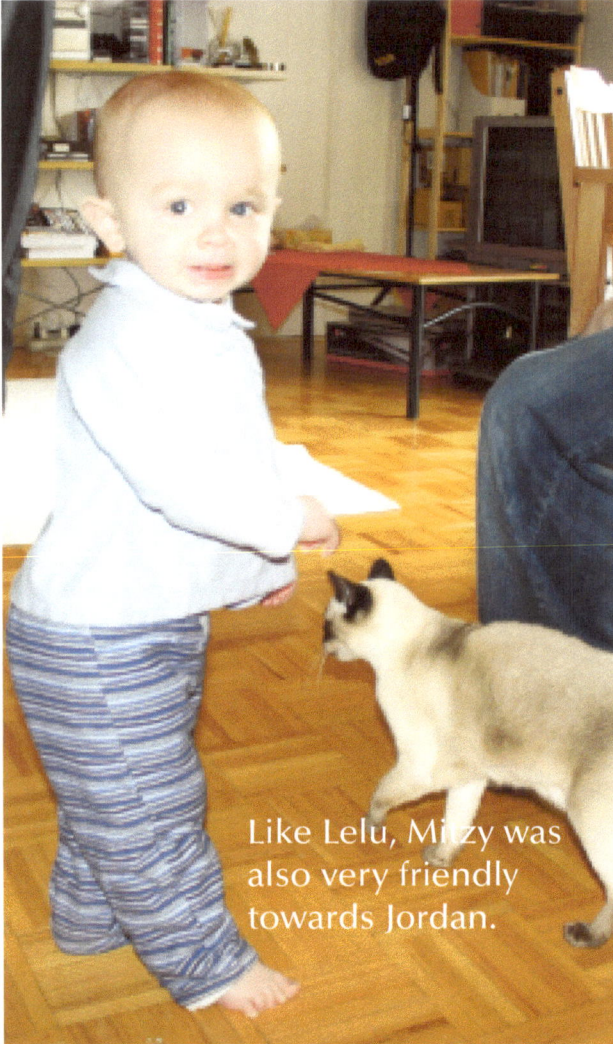

Like Lelu, Mitzy was also very friendly towards Jordan.

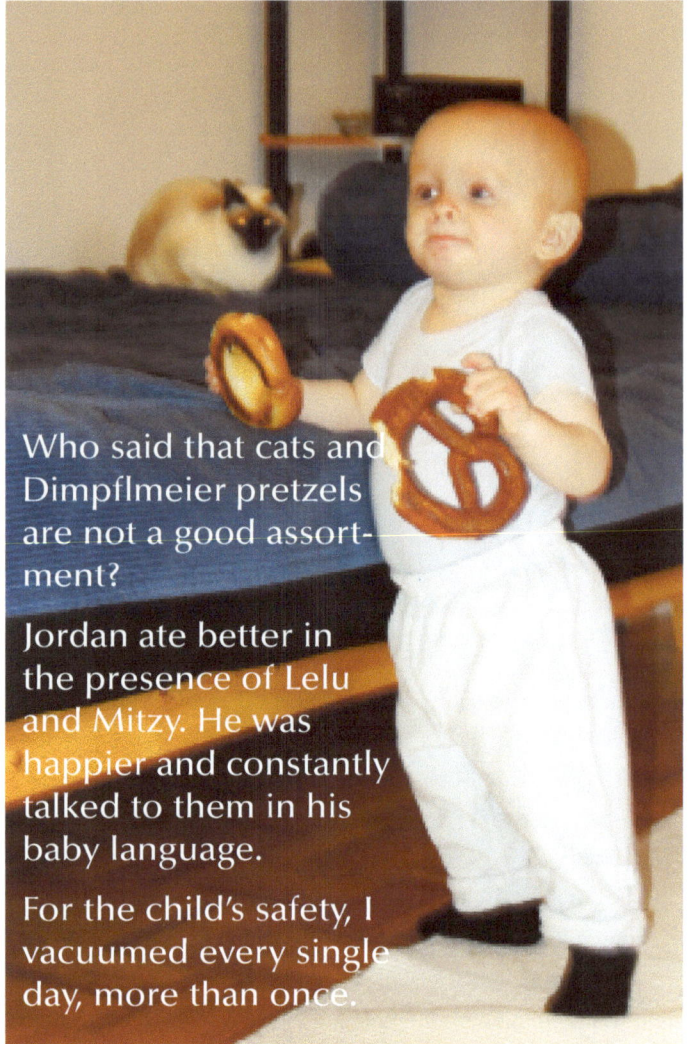

Who said that cats and Dimpflmeier pretzels are not a good assortment?

Jordan ate better in the presence of Lelu and Mitzy. He was happier and constantly talked to them in his baby language.

For the child's safety, I vacuumed every single day, more than once.

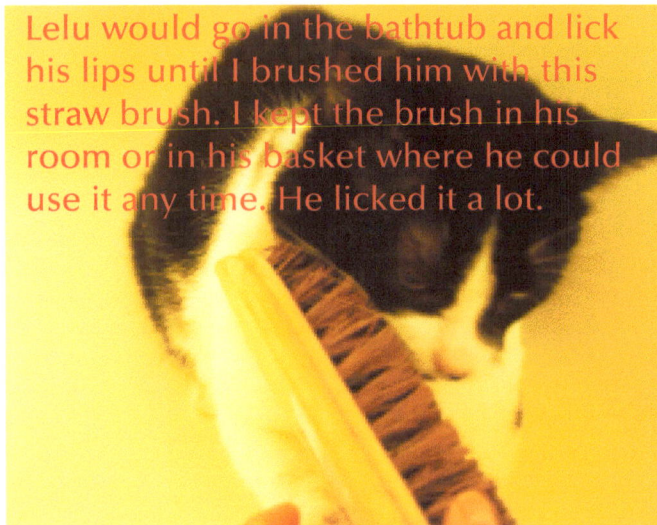

Lelu would go in the bathtub and lick his lips until I brushed him with this straw brush. I kept the brush in his room or in his basket where he could use it any time. He licked it a lot.

Mitzy loved the brush also, but unlike Lelu she did not lick it every day.

Jordan, "Lelu darling ..."

Mitzy streching
a leg.

By next year Jordan grew into a very charming child.

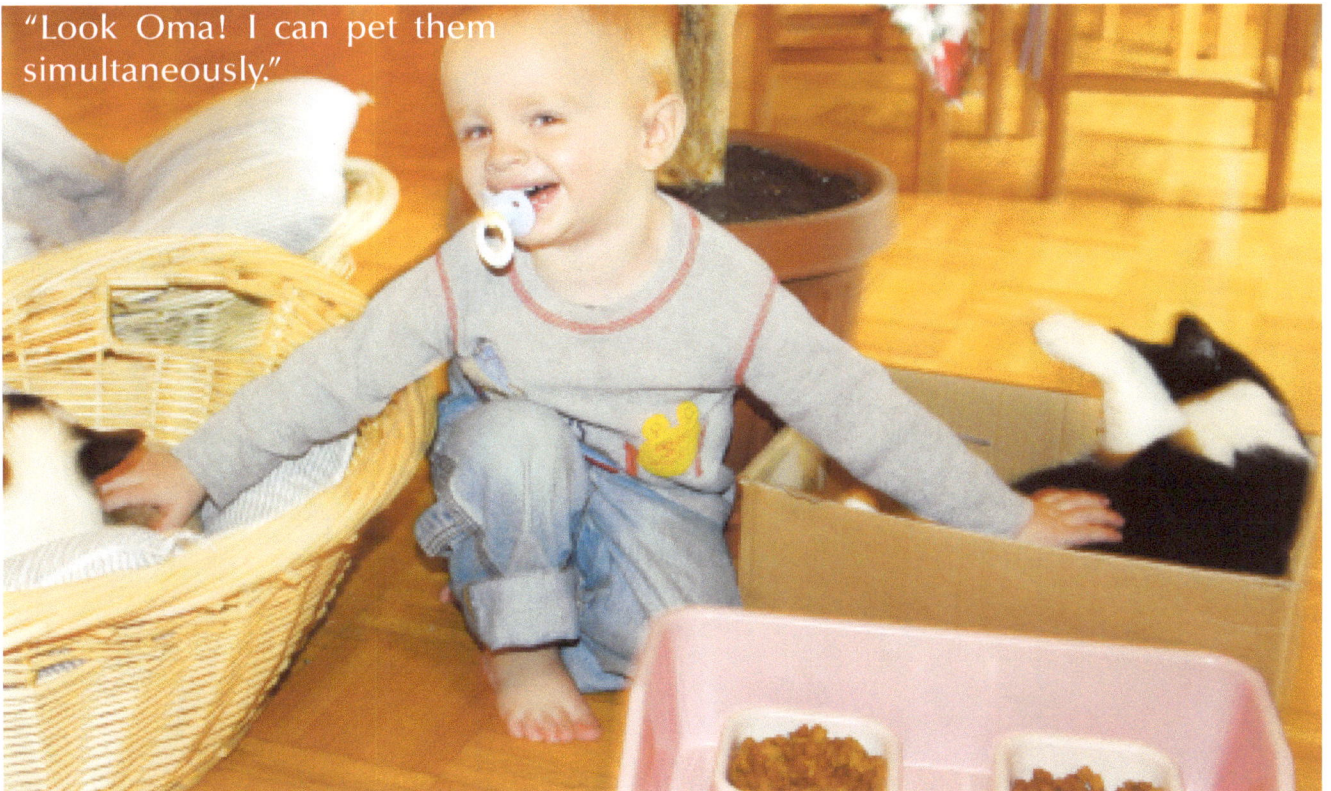

"Look Oma! I can pet them simultaneously."

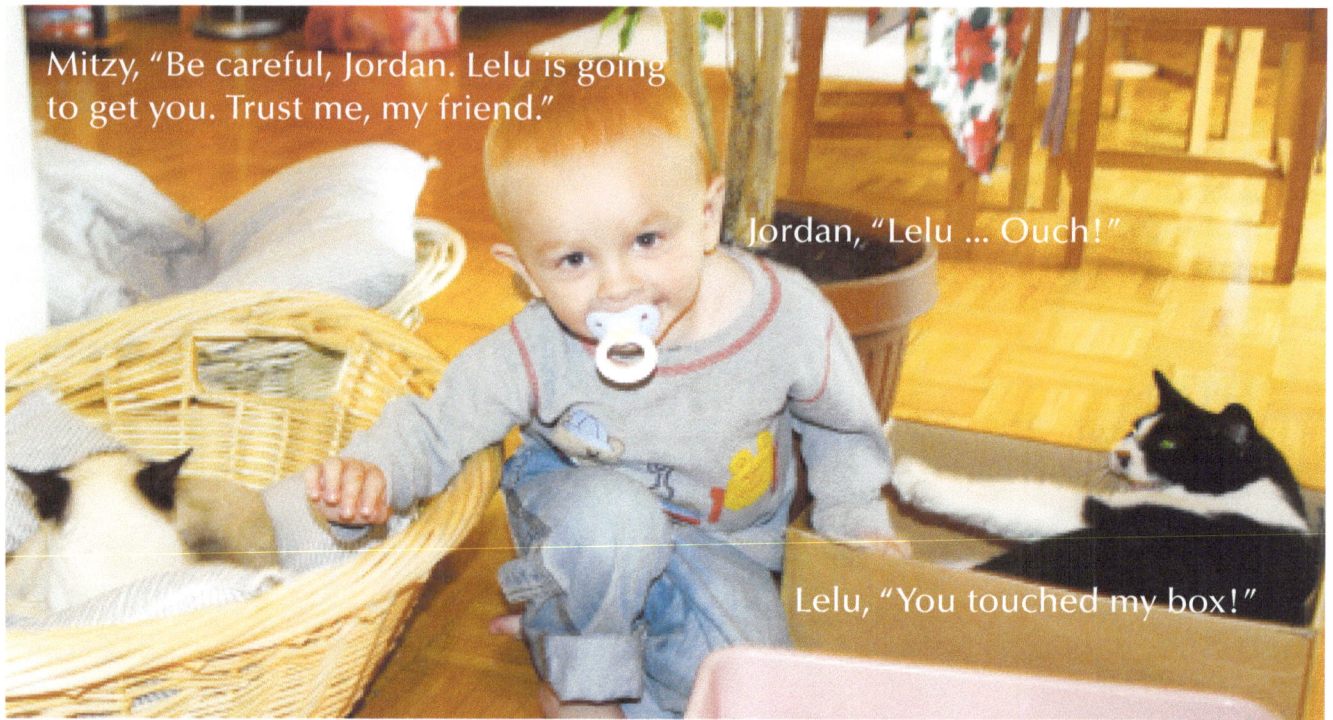

Mitzy, "Be careful, Jordan. Lelu is going to get you. Trust me, my friend."

Jordan, "Lelu ... Ouch!"

Lelu, "You touched my box!"

Jordan, "Oma! Tell Lelu to let go of my sweater."

Mitzy, "See Jordan? I told you so!"

Lelu, "Ha, ha, ha ..."
Oma, "Lelu, please get your nail out of Jordan's sweater."

Yummy! Yummy!

Lelu loved carrots. He would smell them from a distance and he would come running to get them. Fresh carrots were his treats a few times a week.

Lelu would play with a carrot until it was all damaged. Then he would ask for a fresh one.

Lelu, "Hello little insect ... Can I touch you? Are you lost?" Lelu was so gentle ...

Lelu, "If they let us sleep on the corner, that's fine with me."

Lelu in the evening.

On the map of Austria.

Quiet time.

Favourite place.

Round one!

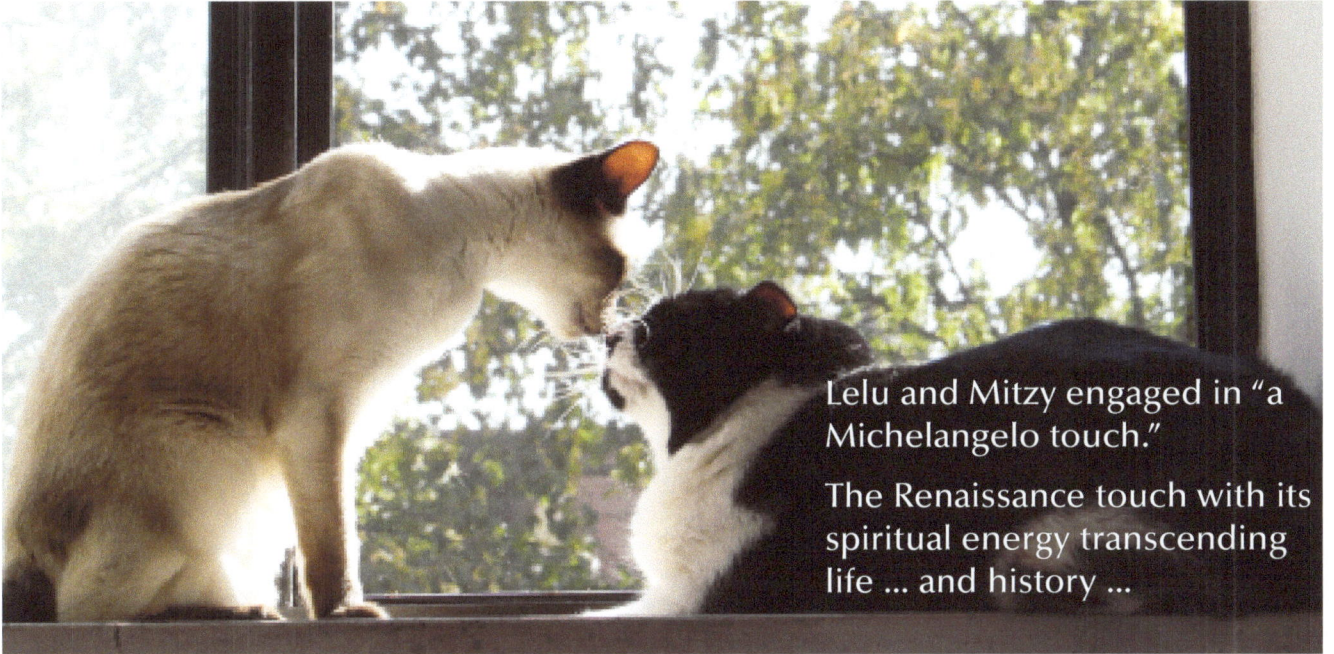

Lelu and Mitzy engaged in "a Michelangelo touch."

The Renaissance touch with its spiritual energy transcending life ... and history ...

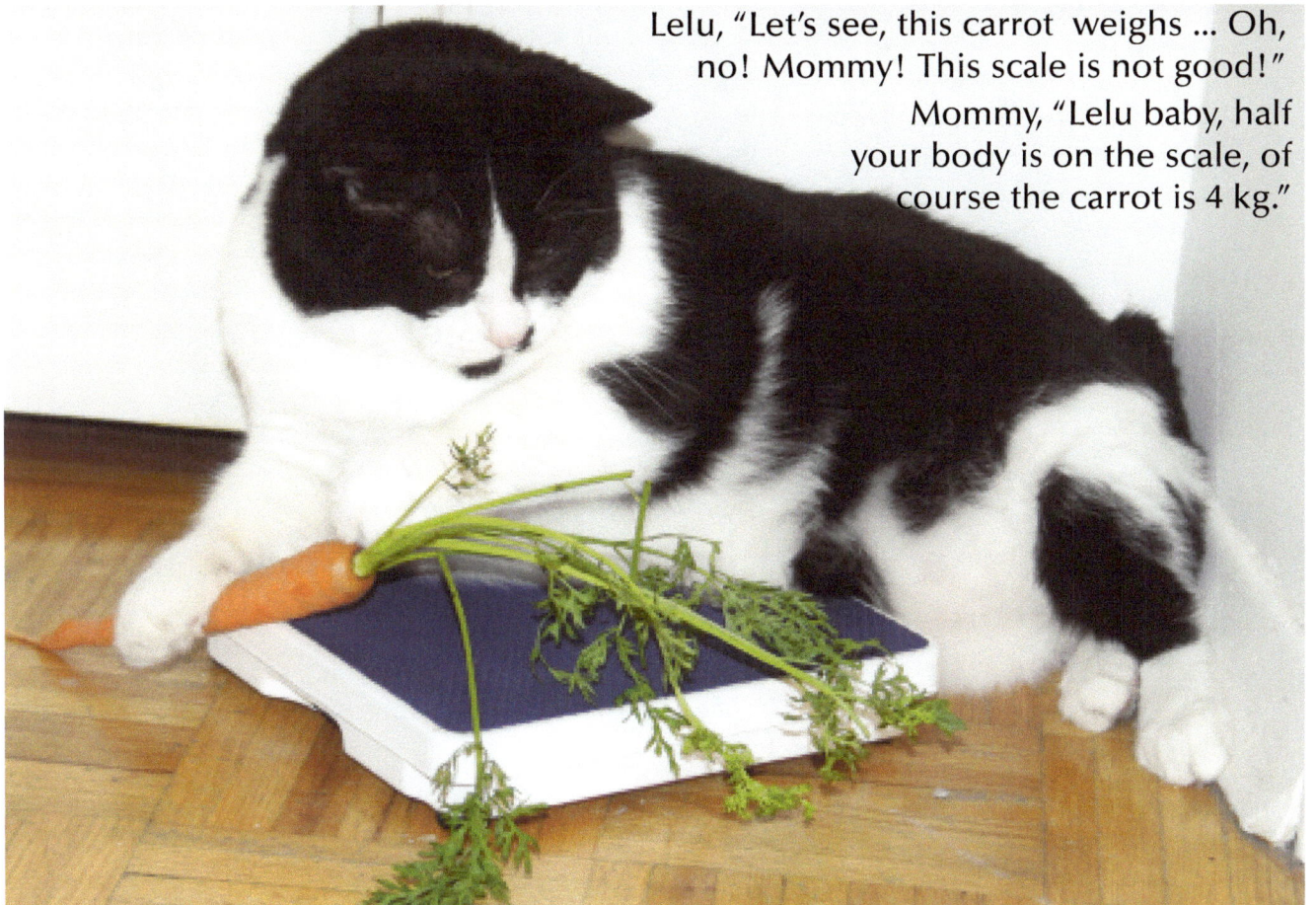

Lelu, "Let's see, this carrot weighs ... Oh, no! Mommy! This scale is not good!"

Mommy, "Lelu baby, half your body is on the scale, of course the carrot is 4 kg."

Playful Lelu, 2007

Jaxson, "Wait Mitzy!"

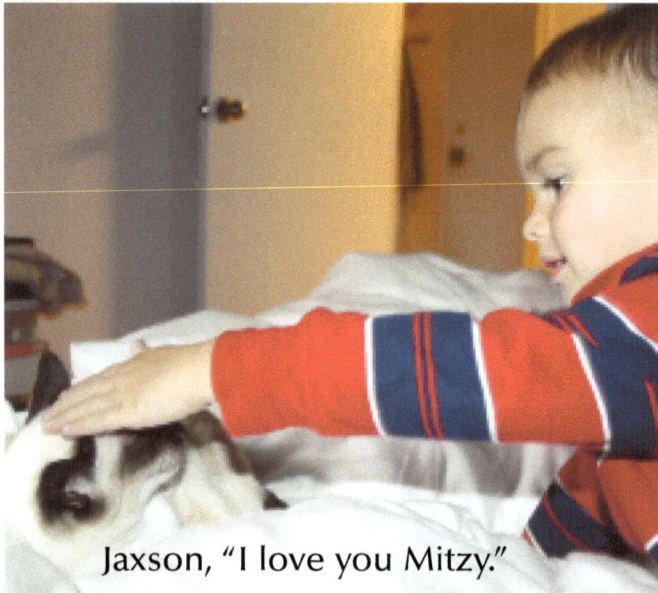

Jaxson, "I love you Mitzy."

Lelu, "Are those real angels?"

Christmas, 2007

Lelu, "Now she took my spot."

Mitzy, "You do not have to walk all over me."

Past bed time,
Lelu, "I think I'll play some more."

At holidays, after guests were gone, peace would set in, and Lelu would once again take over the jungle, until next time.

SENIORITY
ARRIVED

Lelu on the balcony, Feb. '09.

More than half his life Lelu enjoyed living in a house with a garden—the other half in apartments with balconies. There were tall trees all around. Birds and squirrels were everywhere.

Lelu never let Mitzy on the balcony unsupervised. He knew how to take care of her and himself. I always trusted him. If I told him something, he understood, like a human. He was very intelligent.

Mitzy recognized that, and trusted him herself.

Big boy.

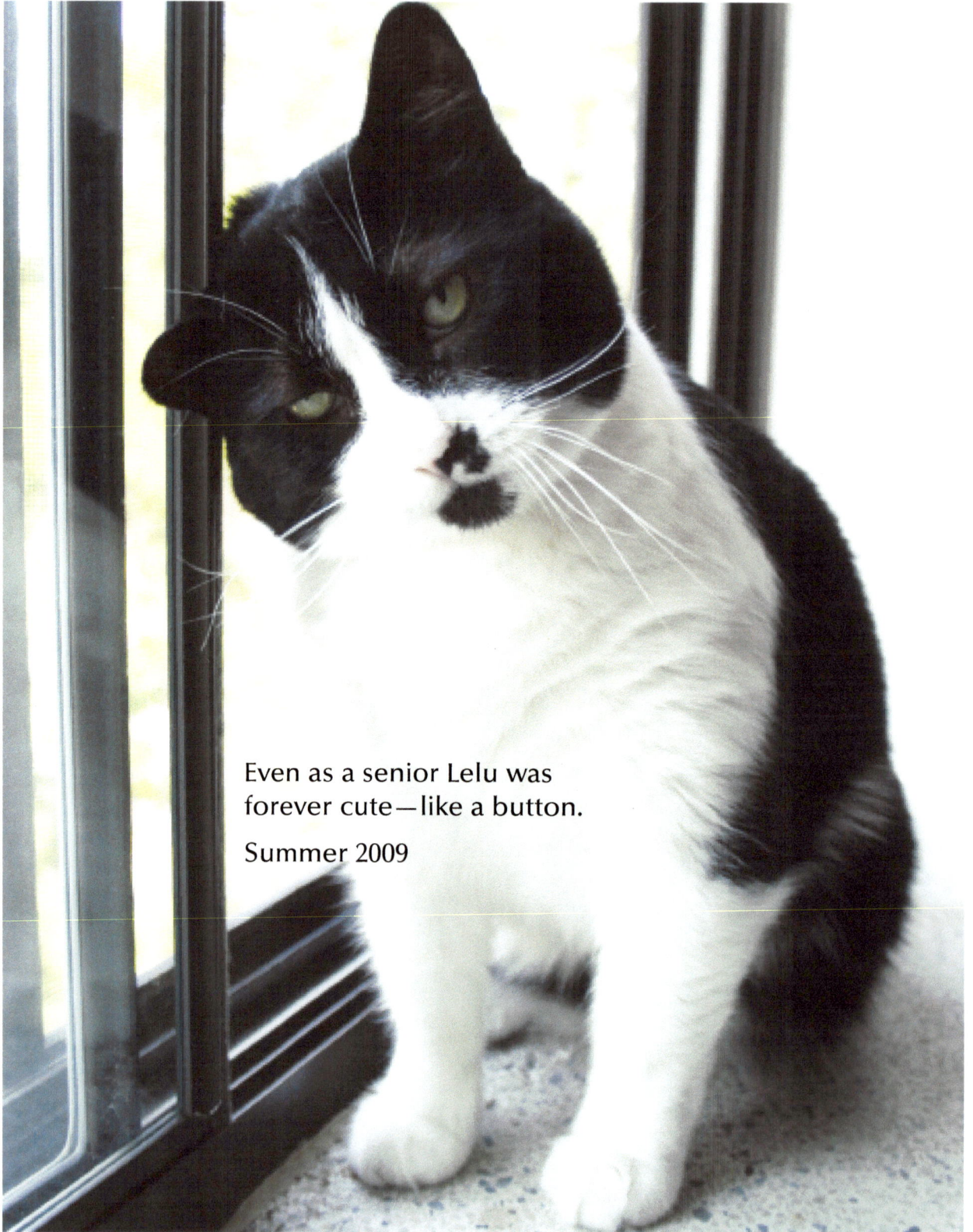

Even as a senior Lelu was
forever cute—like a button.

Summer 2009

Eternal love.
2009

Hi!

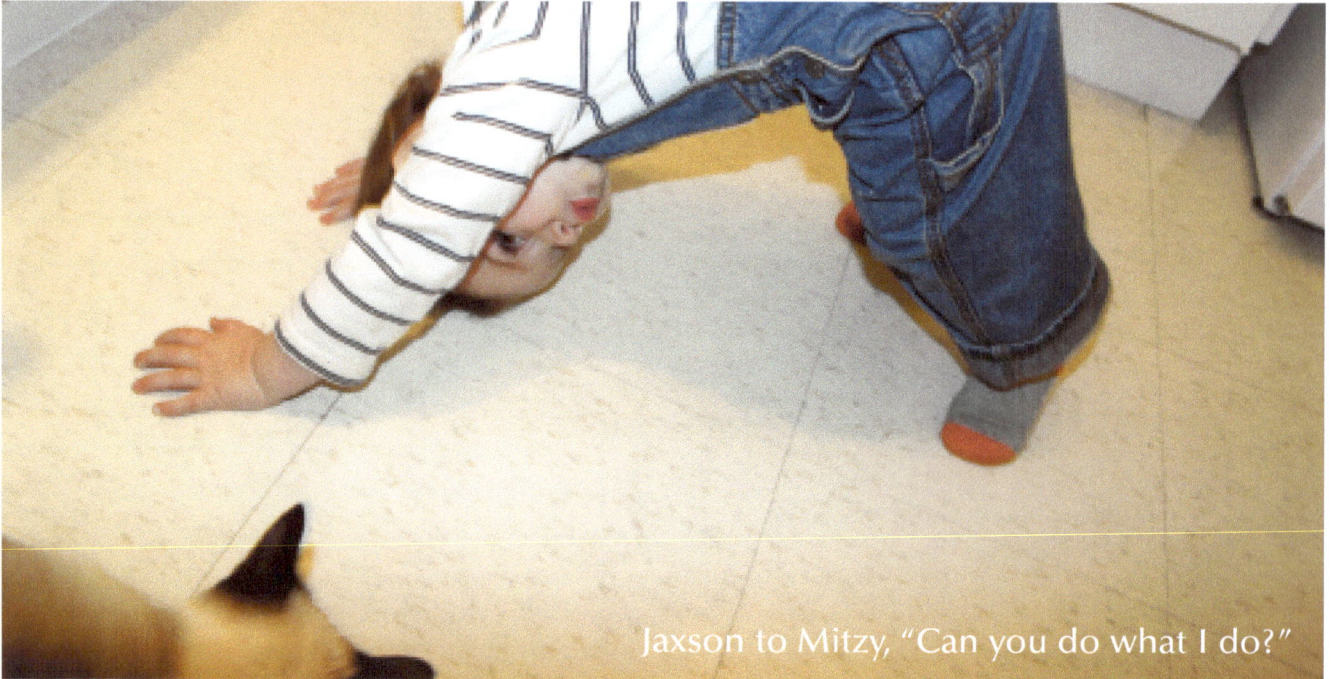

Jaxson to Mitzy, "Can you do what I do?"

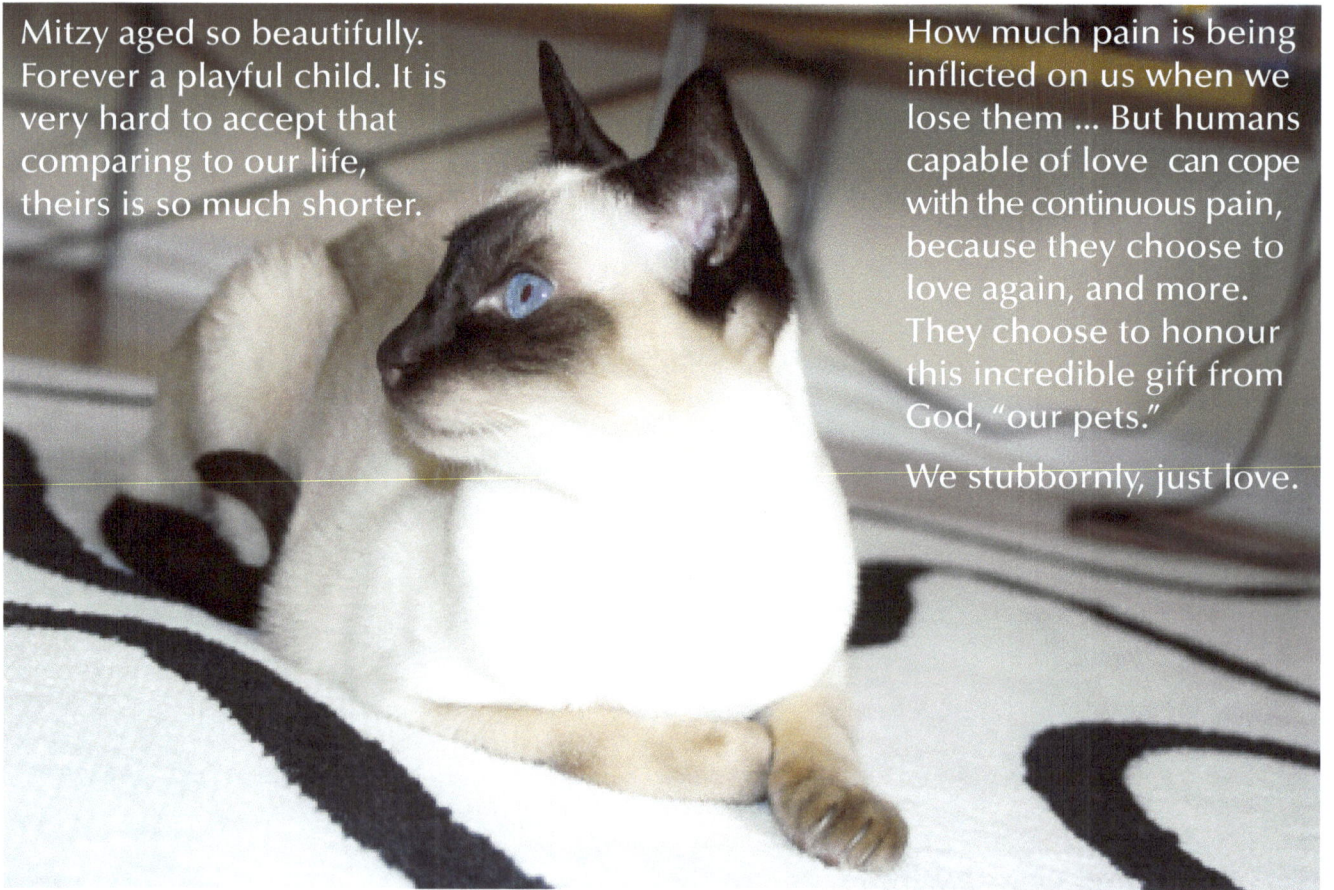

Mitzy aged so beautifully. Forever a playful child. It is very hard to accept that comparing to our life, theirs is so much shorter.

How much pain is being inflicted on us when we lose them ... But humans capable of love can cope with the continuous pain, because they choose to love again, and more. They choose to honour this incredible gift from God, "our pets."

We stubbornly, just love.

Cats or humans, everyone advances in age and try to fit in the shoes of the previous generation. Here, Jordan is thinking, *"I wonder how in the world Oma walks in these big shoes?"*

One day when he will have his own kittens, he will understand.

During the lives of Lelu and Mitzy, Elizabeth become an adult and a mother, three times. Her children enjoyed the cats and grew along loving every moment with them.

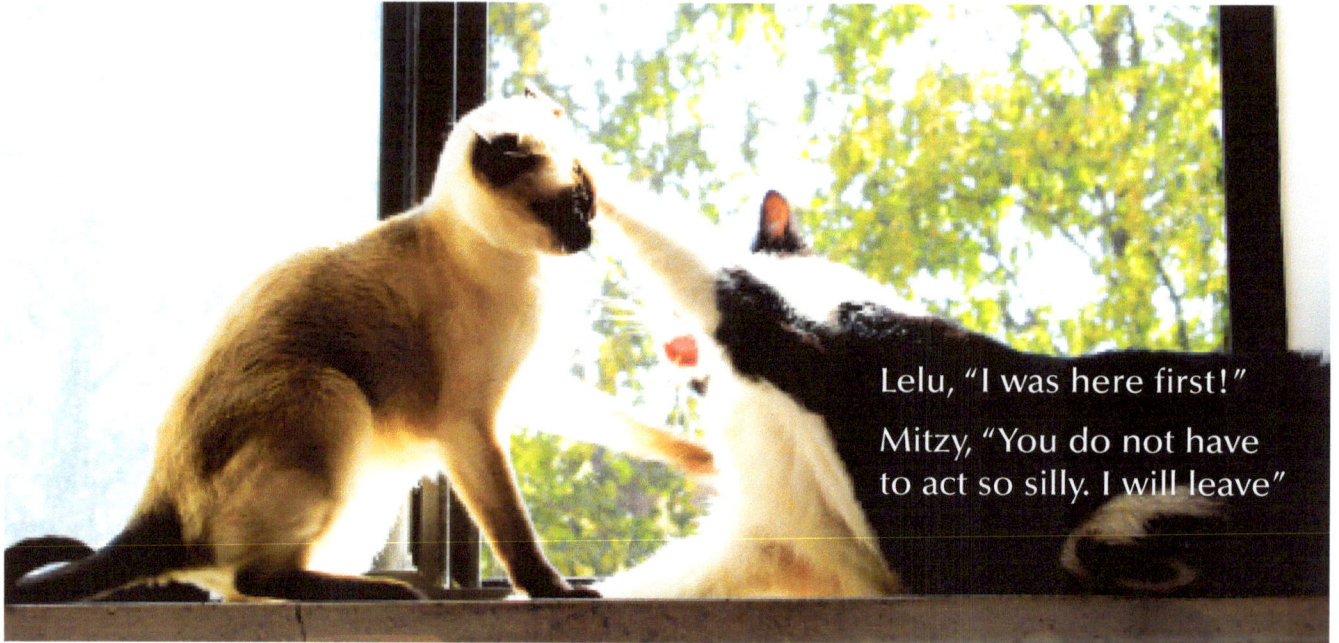

Lelu, "I was here first!"

Mitzy, "You do not have to act so silly. I will leave"

Without Mitzy there, Lelu would stretch to a maximum and meditate ...
Here in the summer of 2009, by now a gentleman enjoying privacy ...

"I'm hungry!"
September 2009, early in the morning on my bed.

November, 2009

Jan. 10, 2010, Lelu & I

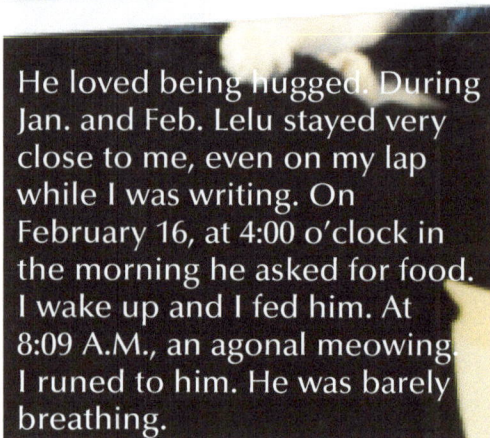

He loved being hugged. During Jan. and Feb. Lelu stayed very close to me, even on my lap while I was writing. On February 16, at 4:00 o'clock in the morning he asked for food. I wake up and I fed him. At 8:09 A.M., an agonal meowing. I runed to him. He was barely breathing.

Winter of 2009-2010. Lelu was happy and charming as usual. Both Lelu and Mitzy loved the wet food. Mitzy started drinking milk again. Lelu started eating home made food, like Mitzy. They could not eat or chew any dry food anymore.

Lelu died in my arms at 8:10 A.M. Feb. 16, 2010. I asked him to fight, but he just could not breathe. Mitzy, agitated, tried to help him also. She stayed there meowing and smelling him. Within a minute, which seemed like an eternity, Lelu's spirit exited his body. I felt it.

"He's gone!" I cried. Then, suddenly the sun came out. A fantasia of snowflakes like a confetti of light started a dance full of finesse, just like Lelu's spirit. A very shiny love-like energy invaded the atmosphere.

"The angels are here!" I sobbed. Inundated by tears I prayed, "Please God—place Lelu in a special paradise. Thank you for his angelic spirit. Thank you for his love."

Mitzy kept vigil. At one point she tried to dig Lelu out of the basket. It really broke my heart to see her in such pain. She loved him so ...

Mitzy would not leave Lelu out of her sight. She sat there, from time to time looking at him in disbelief. She was in shock. She was visibly crying. We waited for a while, giving her the needed time and space. Then we took Lelu's lifeless body for cremation.

To let go of him was extremely traumatic for me. I cried ... When we came back, Mitzy was asleep totally exhausted. Then she refused to eat, drink, play ... She began a phase of mourning. She also started looking for Lelu all over the place, calling him.

A few weeks went by and Mitzy continues calling Lelu. She opens every door. She looks in every box, calling and calling, "Where are you?" she cries even at night. They were so in love ...

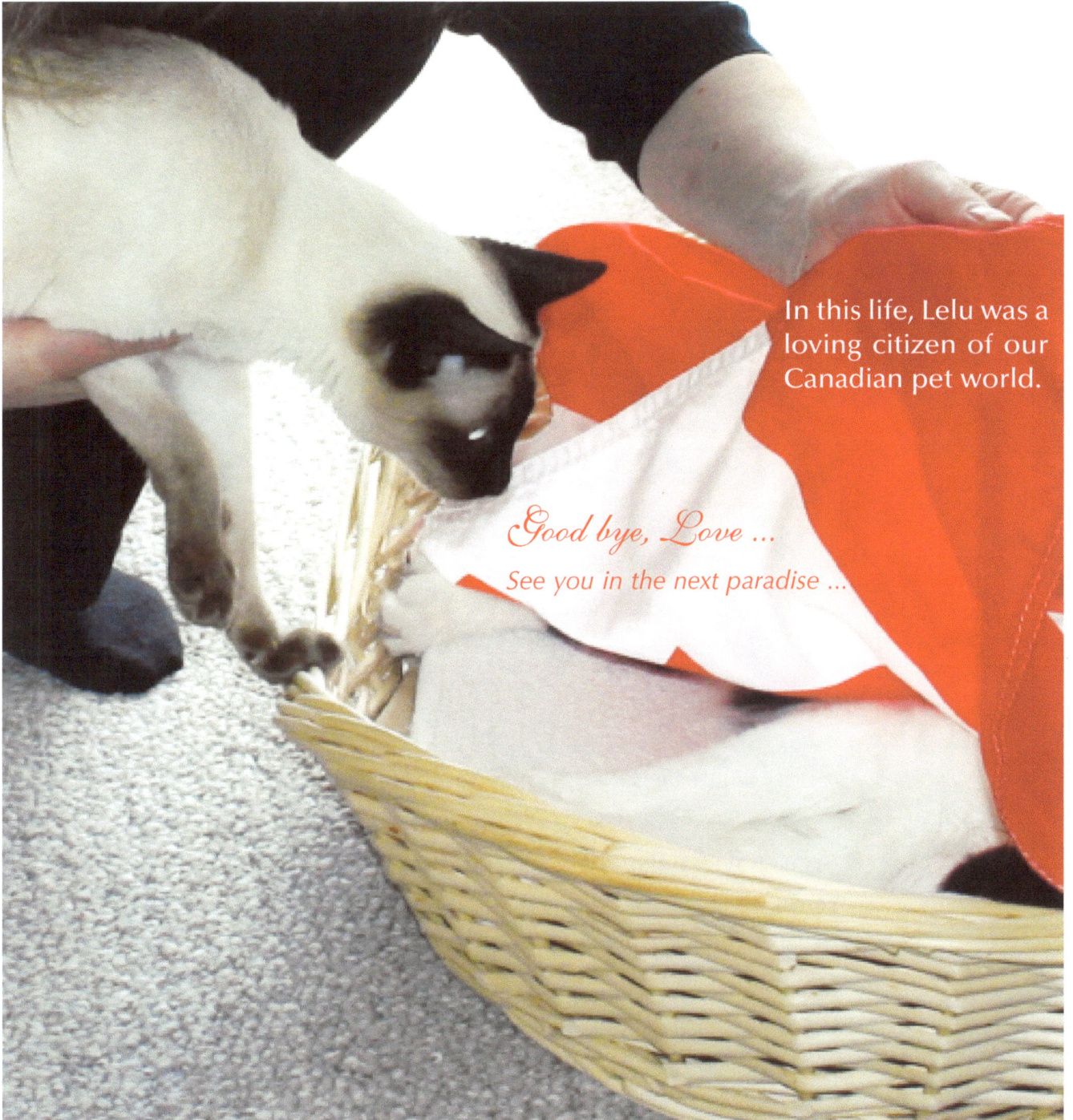

In this life, Lelu was a loving citizen of our Canadian pet world.

Good bye, Love ...

See you in the next paradise ...

Two weeks prior to Lelu's death Mitzy had the premonition. She was howling day and night. For a moment, we thought that she has lost her sanity, but the howling stopped the day Lelu died. In contrast, just prior to his death, Lelu appeared to be more beautiful than ever: loving, shiny coat, good appetite, relaxed, fun ... A loving spirit to the last moment.

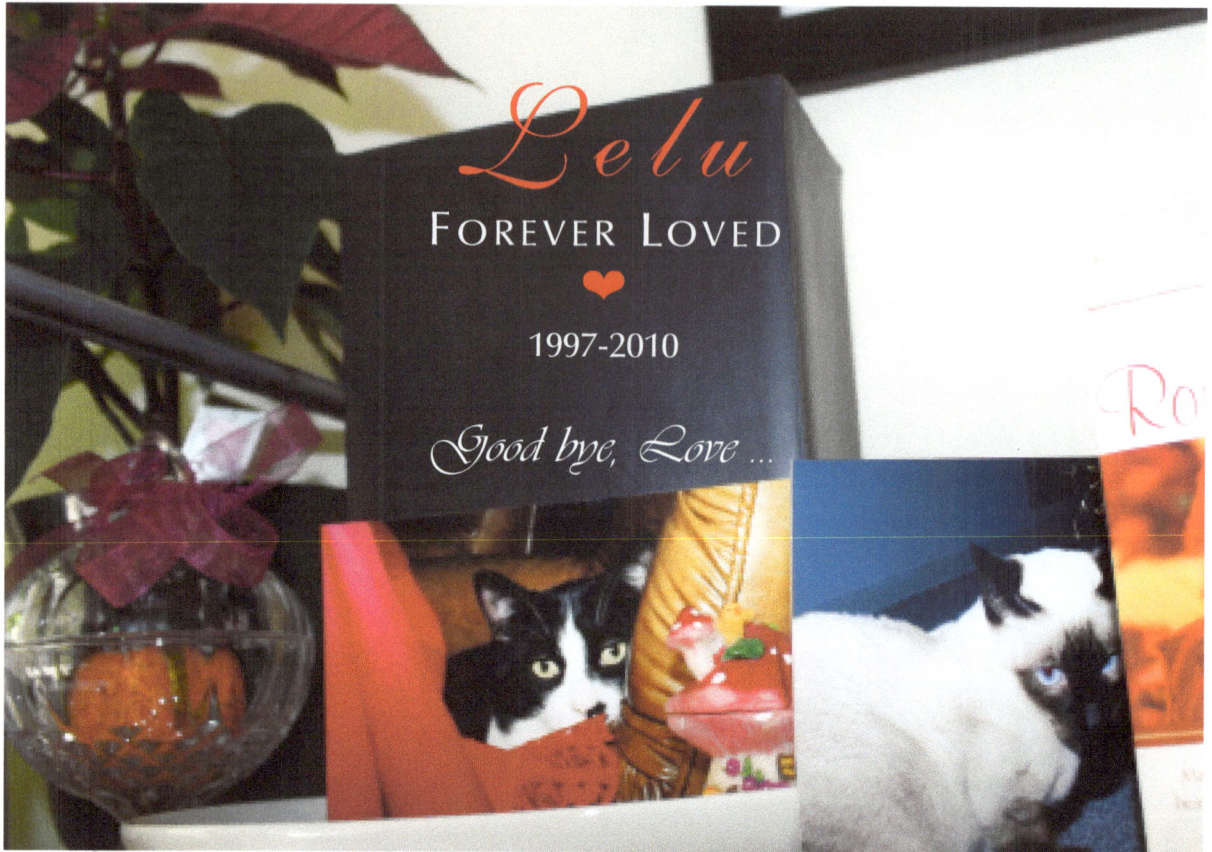

LELU

SPIRIT OF LIGHT, FOREVER—KITTY STAR

FOREVER IS FOREVER—CLOSE OR FAR

YOU LOVED MISS MITZY BEYOND COMPREHENSION

YOUR STORY NOW ATTRACTS THE WORLD'S ATTENTION

I MAGNIFIED YOUR IMAGE IN EACH VERSE

YOU WERE A MANX—YET, YOUR CAT LOVE IMMENSE!

PRESENT FOREVER IN THE UNIVERSE.

I LOVE YOU LELU, VERY MUCH—IT WAS A PRIVILEGE KNOWING YOU IN THIS LIFE.

♥

Elysse

The End

ABOUT THE AUTHOR

Canadian author Elysse Poetis, winner of 2007 Arts Acclaim Award, resides with her husband/publisher in the Region of Waterloo, Ontario, from where she continue her creativity.

www.elyssepoetis.com

BIBLIOGRAPHY
Elysse Poetis

1. **THE MIND OF A POETESS**—*True story, Memoir*
2. **I LOVE YOU**—*CANADIAN Poetry*
3. **FOREVER LOVED**—*A Manx's Cat love story*
4. **THE BEAUTY OF NATURE**—*Photography, Canadian Nature*
5. **FERTILITY GODDESS SOVATA**—*Inspirational*
6. **OPRAH! BEFORE YOU LEAVE ...**—*Novel*
7. **THE HUNTER OF BEAUTY**—*Photography, Canadian Architecture, Landscape, Arts & Entertainment*
8. **GREAT GLOBAL FUN IN CANADA & USA**—*(soon to come)*

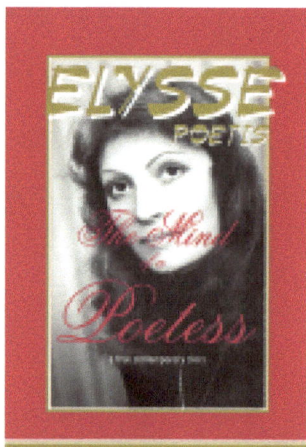

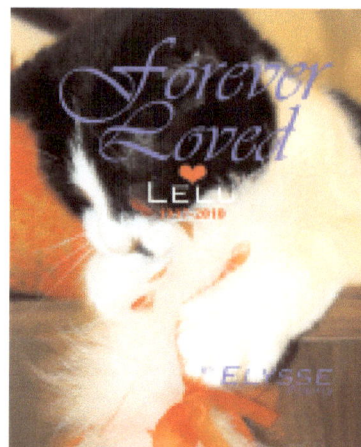

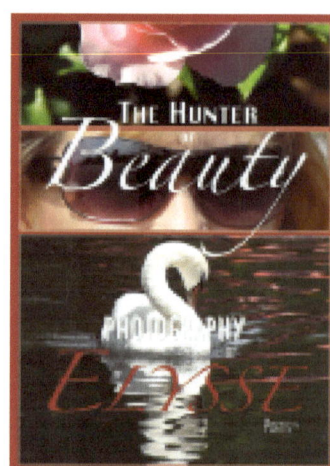

www.ingramcontent.com/pod-product-compliance
Lightning Source LLC
Chambersburg PA
CBHW061054090426

42742CB00002B/41